Clips from the Classroom: *Learning with Technology*

DVD and Activity Guide

Cathy Cavanaugh
University of North Florida

PEARSON
Merrill
Prentice Hall

Upper Saddle River, New Jersey
Columbus, Ohio

Vice President and Executive Publisher: Jeffery W. Johnston
Executive Editor: Debra A. Stollenwerk
Senior Editorial Assistant: Mary Morrill
Development Editor: Amy Nelson
Production Editor: JoEllen Gohr
Design Coordinator: Diane Lorenzo
Cover Designer: Thomas Borah
Cover image: Corbis
Production Manager: Pamela D. Bennett
Director of Marketing: Ann Castel Davis
Marketing Manager: Darcy Betts Prybella
Marketing Coordinator: Brian Mounts

This book was printed and bound by Banta Book Group. The cover was printed by Phoenix Color Corp.

Pearson Education Ltd.
Pearson Education Singapore Pte. Ltd.
Pearson Education Canada, Ltd.
Pearson Education—Japan

Pearson Education Australia Pty. Limited
Pearson Education North Asia Ltd.
Pearson Educación de Mexico, S.A. de C.V.
Pearson Education Malaysia Pte. Ltd.

10 9 8 7 6 5 4 3 2 1
ISBN: 0-13-171274-8

Preface

Introduction

This activity guide and DVD bring you into classrooms and schools where teachers are using technology to improve learning for students across grade levels and content areas. The video clips on the DVD are organized into four sections: Transforming Teaching and Learning, Software and Media, The Internet and Virtual Schools, and Technology across the Curriculum. To prepare you for using technology in your teaching, this guide provides information and activities about getting to know today's students (knowledge), planning for technology-enhanced learning (skills), and continuing your development as a technology-using educator (professional dispositions, values, commitments, and ethics). The book also guides your visits to the classrooms on the DVD with activities and reflection questions. Each teacher featured on the DVD shares unique viewpoints, practices, and styles as a master technology-using educator.

Technology-enhanced teaching and learning

There are many ways to use technology to enhance teaching and learning. When access to technology is limited, students can learn from technology-delivered presentations and text that they or their teachers produce. Teachers can perform some of the management tasks of their jobs more efficiently by using technology such as electronic grade book software, telecommunications, or word processing. When technology is available for hands-on work, teachers and students can use technology to learn in new and different ways to do things they wouldn't otherwise be able to do, like visualize and interact with simulations of unreachable times and places in multiple dimensions. Each of these uses of technology in education offers different benefits and reflects different conceptions of the purpose of technology in education.

Technology can support, enhance, and transform the teaching and learning processes, depending on how it is used. Technology-enhanced teaching and learning happens when technology is used in ways that benefits students and leads to improved educational outcomes. Because "the success or failure of technology is more dependent on human and contextual factors than on hardware or software" (Valdez et al., 2000), this book focuses less on the hardware, software, and infrastructure, and more on the instructional vision and informed judgment of the teacher, who develops knowledge of when and why to use the technology.

Organization of the text

This guide provides information about the technical steps for using the features of the DVD. It also includes contextual information and guiding activities to use before and after viewing video segments. The guide contains five chapters.

The first chapter, Learning with Technology in Action, describes each teacher featured in the video segments. An introduction to the teacher is followed by an overview of the concepts shown in the segment and questions to guide your thinking and reflection about the segment. Chapter 2, Getting to Know the Students in Today's Schools, introduces you to the students who are learning in today's classrooms. You'll get to know how they think, how they learn, and the role of technology in their lives and education. Chapter 3, Effective Technology for Today's Students, provides strategies and rationale for choosing technology for teaching. Benefits and cautions for using educational technology are discussed, and methods for evaluating technology are included. Chapter 4, Planning for Technology in Teaching and Learning, focuses on planning for teaching with technology. It describes professional development approaches for teachers who want to use the most effective technology to enhance student learning, and it offers guidance for preparing technology-enhanced lessons and units. The fifth chapter, Expanding the Classroom with Technology, highlights ways that teachers are using technology to involve families and the community in student learning.

The Resources section presents a collection of materials, including assessment rubrics, sample responses to reflection questions, and bibliographic and web references.

DVD video themes

Four themes are used on the DVD to organize the video segments. The segments were filmed in elementary, middle, and high schools, and in a K-12 school for students who are deaf and blind. They show teaching in social studies, mathematics, science, English language arts, foreign languages, visual arts, and music. The students represent diverse cultural, ethnic, linguistic, and socioeconomic backgrounds, as well as a range of academic abilities in grades 1-12.

- **Theme 1: Transforming Teaching and Learning.** Here we see teachers in two schools where innovative, creative, and thoughtful uses of technology have changed the ways that students are learning and teachers are teaching. Valarie Young invites us into her high school World History classroom at the Advanced Technology Academy in Las Vegas, Nevada. In Valarie's class a range of technology is seamlessly integrated into the classroom culture. Therese Keith, mother of one of Valarie's students, tells us about the importance of technology for her son. Mary Lynn Smith and her high school Spanish students at the Bolles School in Jacksonville, Florida, have learned to use technology to make their class more engaging and interactive. Mary Lynn's colleagues join together in a conversation about how technology has changed their role in their classrooms.

- **Theme 2: Software and Media.** We visit four schools in the second section. Shelly Couch and Amy Eisler take us inside their 5th grade classrooms at Cunningham Creek Elementary School in Jacksonville, Florida. They teach science and mathematics to students who use software tools on their own laptop computers. We follow a group of 6th grade students on their expedition into SpaceLab at the Challenger Center in Jacksonville, made possible by using simulation software. In Mike Patterson's high school geometry class at the Advanced Technology Academy, students use mathematics modeling software as part of an inquiry learning experience. In the 1st and 4th grade classrooms of Jennifer Salley and Caryn Canfield at the Bolles School, students learn social studies and subtraction by creating their own presentations and then sharing them with the class using tablet computers.

- **Theme 3: The Internet and Virtual Schools.** In this section, two virtual schools and two school-based classrooms are featured. At the Odyssey Charter School in Las Vegas, high school and middle school students meet together on campus with teachers once each week, and learn by using the communications capabilities of the Internet for the rest of the week. At the Florida Virtual School, based in Orlando, Florida, students in grades 6-12 take classes completely online. In the classrooms of Valarie Young and Mike Patterson, the Internet is used in the classroom during large group activities and as a rich source of information for small group and independent student learning.

- **Theme 4: Technology across the Curriculum.** In this section, we explore a range of strategies used by teachers in six different academic areas and in classrooms for students with special needs. Each teacher uses technology in unique and effective ways, depending on the individual teaching style, the demands of the content, and the learning needs of the students. Patty Kmieciak's high school students at the Bolles School are thoroughly engaged in her literature lesson in part because of her use of multimedia. Kate Pritchard's students at the Episcopal High School of Jacksonville use language lab software that provides them with extended time for guided practice in dialogue. Mike Patterson's high school trigonometry students use a discovery learning approach aided by graphing calculators. Don Page uses the software tools of the tablet computer to draw his high school students at the Bolles School into the Trojan Wars. Richard Chamberlain's photography students at Episcopal analyze work shown on an Internet gallery, and then they apply their knowledge to their own digital photos. Lynn Howard's students at Episcopal use music composition software to compose and play original pieces that demonstrate their understanding of music concepts. Colette Cook and Teresa Smith use SmartBoards with their elementary and middle school students at the Florida School for the Deaf and Blind in St. Augustine, Florida. The technology enables hands-on practice with language skills to students who are deaf and hard of hearing.

Features
To better understand the practice of technology-enhanced teaching and learning, you are provided with supports in this book.
- Each chapter connects to National Educational Technology Standards for Teachers (NETS-T)
- Each video teaching example is linked to NETS for both teachers and students.
- Each chapter includes questions and activities.
- This activity guide includes a bibliography and a "webliography" for further study.

Acknowledgments

In the process of working on this project, we met a capable, caring, and committed group of educational professionals who graciously invited us into their classrooms, both real and virtual. Each of the teachers cares as much about teaching the next generation of teachers who will learn from this film as they do about teaching the next generation of citizens in their classrooms. To them we are grateful:

Heidi Allen
Craig Butz
Caryn Canfield
Robert Carter
Richard Chamberlain
Colette Cook
Shelly Couch
Amy Eisler
Lynn Howard
Sheree Kearns
Therese Keith
Patty Kmieciak
Don Page
Mike Patterson
Kate Pritchard
Don Reott
Jennifer Salley
April Schmidt
Mary Lynn Smith
Teresa Smith
Valarie Young

Clips from the Classroom: Learning with Technology DVD and Activity Guide

CONTENTS

To the Reader

Consider the role that technology plays in your life. You may be a technophile who depends on a laptop or desktop computer, a cell phone, a handheld computer, and other chip-driven devices for communication, organization, productivity, information, entertainment, and creative activities. Even if you are a technophobe who tends to avoid technology in your own life, you depend on the technology around you to manage transportation, medical care, commerce, media, and other aspects of life. When asked to name an occupation in which technology is not used today, most people can name just a few jobs.

Technology is powerful. It has enormous potential, including the ability to help students learn in new and deeper ways. Using technology in classrooms requires change: physical change in the infrastructure of schools, change in staffing to manage the technology, change in how students approach their learning, and change in how teachers approach teaching. Technology is not perfect, and it is not always easy, but it is becoming ubiquitous and necessary in education.

This book and DVD will introduce you to teachers and students who have successfully embraced technology in their classrooms. It will show you reasons for learning to use technology in teaching, and methods for teaching with technology. When you see and hear the students and teachers shown here, you will feel their passion, excitement, and success, and you will know why the change is worthwhile.

What Is Technology?

Technology has existed for as long as people have used tools. Technology is broadly defined as an innovation, modification, or application of knowledge to solve problems or meet human needs. Educators have been especially adept at adopting technology for teaching. Recall that the book, pen, chalkboard, overhead projector, and television were all once new to classrooms. They have now become an inseparable part of the education experience, each adding a new, valuable capability to the classroom. Digital technology is the new learning technology of our generation.

Becoming an Effective Technology-Using Educator

It is hard to imagine a future in which technology does not play an increasingly central part in life. Technology affords individuals access to an unimaginable wealth of information that improves quality of life. Technology skills open doors to an expanded range of careers. Technology increases every student's menu of education choices, and extends his or her abilities as a learner. Technology adds efficiency to the bureaucratic tasks of teachers. In short, there are many reasons to become a technology-using educator.

The most effective technology-using educators have the following dispositions:
- An open mind about the benefits that technology can offer professionally and personally
- Confidence about being able to learn to use new technology
- A belief in the value of lifelong learning for everyone
- A sense of pride in being a learner in the classroom alongside students, and sometimes learning from students
- Trust in a network of professional contacts to ask for assistance, advice, and support
- A creative approach to designing lessons

- Excitement about the potential of new technology
- Recognition of the importance of technology in their students' lives
- Knowledge that their colleagues are among their most valuable resources

Welcome to *Clips from the Classroom: Learning with Technology*

Each teacher finds unique ways to use classroom resources that work with his or her own teaching style. Just as not every teacher uses the chalkboard in the same ways or for the same amount of time, not every teacher uses the same technologies in the same ways. Fortunately, teachers are professional sharers—they can be counted on to teach each other. The teachers and students you see on this DVD have volunteered to teach you, and there are many like them in schools everywhere. Such teachers will be honored when you ask them to share what works in their classrooms. This guide and DVD are a jumping-off point designed to get you started on a path of effective technology-enabled teaching. We believe you can learn something new about good teaching from each teacher featured here, and we are certain you will someday share your skills with another teacher.

GETTING STARTED WITH THE DVD

USERS' GUIDE FOR
CLIPS FROM THE CLASSROOM: LEARNING WITH TECHNOLOGY

Installation and Use Instructions

DVD Deck Operation
1. Insert DVD in tray. Wait for a short time while the program loads.
2. The title and main menu screen will appear ready for you to make a selection.
3. Using the remote control, switch the remote to DVD operation.
4. Using the arrow keys on the remote, scroll through the menu study titles and navigation button located in the lower, right-hand portion of the screen that says "Next". The right and lower arrow keys will scroll down and the left and upper arrow keys will scroll up.
5. The study or the navigation button that is selected at any given time will turn the color red. If you press "Enter" on the remote, the content on the screen will change.
6. The screen now will show the submenu for a particular study and the navigation buttons in the lower, right-hand portion of the screen.
7. Once again, using the arrow keys on the remote, scroll through the various video clip titles and/or navigation buttons.
8. Pushing the "Enter" button on the remote will cause a video clip to play. If a navigation button is selected (and turns red), it will take you to the main menu or another study menu.
9. Once a video clip is playing, the remote controls can be used to Stop, Pause, Fast Forward, Fast Reverse, or return to the Main Menu.
10. While video clips are playing, the arrow keys on the remote control can also be used to skip to the next video clip within a study or skip back to the previous video clip in the same study.

Computer Operation
1. Insert DVD in the CD-ROM.DVD tray. Wait for a short time while the program loads automatically. If the DVD does not load automatically on the PC, then open a DVD player such as Windows Media Player. For Windows Media Player, go to Start (lower left-hand corner), then All Programs, then find Windows Media Player in the programs list. Other DVD players such as Inter Actual Player or InterVideo WinDVD 4 may also be available in the list. Double-click on the player image to open it. Then click on the Play button and the DVD should open to the first screen. A DVD on Macintosh computers usually opens automatically, but in the case it does not, then go to the DVD player in the Application folder on the hard disk and open it manually. From there on, the program should open to the first screen.
2. The title and main menu screen will appear ready for you to make a selection.
3. To view full screen, click on the full screen button with the computer mouse. The full screen button is located in the lower right-hand corner of the viewing screen in Windows Media Player. Every player has this option, but the controlling buttons are in different locations. Each player's Help section may be of use.

4. Using the computer mouse or the keyboard arrow keys, scroll through the menu study titles and navigation button located in the lower right-hand portion of the screen that says "Next." The right and lower arrow keys will scroll down and the left and upper arrow keys will scroll up.

5. The study or the navigation button that is selected at any given time will turn the color red. If you press "Enter" on the keyboard or click with the mouse on the red-colored title or navigation button, the content on the screen will change.

6. The screen now will show the submenu for a particular study and the navigation buttons in the lower right-hand portion of the screen.

7. Once again, using the arrow keys on the computer keyboard or the computer mouse, scroll through the various video clip titles and/or navigation buttons.

8. Pushing the "Enter" button on the keyboard or clicking with the mouse on the video clip title will cause a video clip to play. If a navigation button is selected, it will take you to the main menu or another study menu.

9. Once a video clip is playing, the player controls can be used to Stop, Pause, Fast Forward, Fast Reverse, or return to the Main Menu.

10. While video clips are playing, the skip buttons on the player control can also be used to skip to the next video clip within a study or skip back to the previous video clip in the same study.

11. Push the Esc button on the computer keyboard to end the program.

CHAPTER 1
LEARNING WITH TECHNOLOGY IN ACTION

THEME 1: Transforming Teaching and Learning

Students in today's schools are different from students attending school during past generations. Their lives, interests, and abilities have changed as a result of changes in society. Teachers have changed their practice, too, and some of the change is related to technology. Throughout the *Clips from the Classroom* DVD, you will see teachers who have changed their teaching to better meet the needs of their students by using technology. In the clips listed below, two teachers have invited us into their classrooms to see the effects of transformed teaching on student learning.

Below is a list of the ten clips related to Transforming Teaching and Learning. Please watch these clips before considering the discussion and reflection questions that follow.

Student Achievement Increases.
Student motivation and engagement are evident in Valarie Young's class, and she has seen her students' achievement increase as she has transformed her teaching to use more technology. Valarie teaches high school world history at the Advanced Technology Academy in Las Vegas, Nevada.

Technology Improves Teaching Skills.
Valarie Young is a relative newcomer to classroom technology integration. She developed skills as a result of several professional development experiences, and she sees herself as a lifelong learner.

Technology Manages Flow of Activities.
On a typical day in Valarie's class, students learn by using the Internet, digital video, and presentations, among other technology. The technology supports learning that alternates between directed and constructivist approaches.

Assessment Examples Illustrated.
Valarie uses multiple strategies to assess her students' learning when they use a range of technology with other classroom resources. Her students are learning Greek history with multimedia, and Valarie gives examples of the assessments she uses to be sure her students meet the content standards for the course.

Secondary Students Respond Positively.
Valarie has seen changes in her own teaching as well as in the learning of her students since she began teaching with technology in her social studies classes. In her classes, there is a seamless flow among the technologies and other materials used by students.

PowerPoint Guides and Prompts Teaching.
One of Valarie's challenges in teaching with technology has been selecting the technology that is appropriate to the learning situation. Her students are engaged in their world history lesson in part because of the multimedia presentations Valarie has designed.

Parent Pleased with Son's Opportunities.
Therese Keith's son attends the Advanced Technology Academy in Las Vegas. He selected the technology magnet school to help him achieve personal and professional goals. His success is made possible by the shared vision of students, parents, teachers, and administrators who recognize the value of technology for learning, and who have made a commitment to create a culture supportive of innovative uses of technology.

Tablet Computers Facilitate Learning.
A group of high school teachers at the Bolles School in Jacksonville, Florida, has just begun using tablet computers with their students. Each teacher has developed a unique approach for integrating the technology to complement his or her teaching style, content area, and students.

Students Discuss Tablet Use.
Students at the Bolles School have benefited from their school's innovative use of technology. They discuss examples from their courses.

Tablet Computers in Spanish.
Mary Lynn Smith integrates her tablet computer as an interactive tool for teaching and learning Spanish at the Bolles School. Scenes from her classroom show the interactive and engaging potential of the tablet and projector.

Discussion Questions

1. Technology is used in teaching and learning for many purposes, such as increasing student interest and motivation for learning, increasing student time spent interacting with content, addressing a fuller range of student learning styles, providing professional tools for student work, and helping students to develop skills in evaluation and communication. What are some of the benefits the students get from technology in the classrooms shown in the clips?

2. Valarie Young and Mary Lynn Smith chose technology to address learning problems that they identified in their classes. Describe a learning problem from one of the classes, and explain how technology was used in the solution to the problem.

3. Technology is best used in a classroom when it has a relative advantage over a non-technology approach. Select a technology in use in one of the classrooms shown in the clips, and discuss the advantage that the technology has over teaching without the technology.

Reflection Questions

1. Any transformation requires certain knowledge, skills, and dispositions (professional values, commitments, and ethics). For example, transforming a health course to include student production of a digital video documenting community health issues would require knowledge of the issues and students' abilities with the technology, skill in coordinating community resources and using the technology to create and produce video, and the disposition that the students are

capable of learning the skills necessary for the project. After watching Valarie Young or Mary Lynn Smith, give examples of the knowledge, skills, and dispositions they needed to transform their teaching.

2. When beginning to use a new technology tool in a classroom, teachers may face barriers that influence the initial implementation of the technology. Effective technology use usually happens in stages. What are some of the barriers Valarie Young or Mary Lynn Smith might have overcome to reach the stage of effectiveness we see in these clips?

3. The clip "Parent Pleased with Son's Opportunities" features a parent discussing her support of technology in her son's education. What might be a parent's reasons for supporting classroom technology? What might be his or her reasons not to support it?

4. The technology that is used in the schools featured in the clips is there because of a vision of what is possible. It took hard work to put the technology in place, and we can see the payoff in the students. What vision do you have for what students may someday be able to do with technology? What steps can a teacher take to realize a technology vision for his or her classroom?

National Educational Technology Standards for Students (NETS-S) Question

1. In the classrooms where tablet computers are used, students are using technology tools for learning. For each of the following clips give an example of how students are meeting NETS-S standard 3: "to enhance learning, increase productivity, and promote creativity."

National Educational Technology Standards for Teachers (NETS-T) and for Students (NETS-S) addressed in the clips:

a.   "Tablet Computers Facilitate Learning"

b.   "Students Discuss Tablet Use"

c.   "Tablet Computers in Spanish"

Theme 1 DVD Clips: Transforming Teaching and Learning	NETS-T	NETS-S
Technology Improves Teaching Skills	**I. TECHNOLOGY OPERATIONS AND CONCEPTS.** Teachers: a. demonstrate introductory knowledge, skills, and understanding of concepts related to technology (as described in the ISTE National Education Technology Standards for Students) b. demonstrate continual growth in technology knowledge and skills to stay abreast of current and emerging technologies.	NA
Student Achievement Increases	**III. TEACHING, LEARNING, AND THE CURRICULUM.** Teachers: d. manage student learning activities in a technology-enhanced environment.	NA
Technology Manages Flow of Activities	**II. PLANNING AND DESIGNING LEARNING ENVIRONMENTS AND EXPERIENCES.** Teachers: d. plan for the management of technology resources within the context of learning activities. e. plan strategies to manage student learning in a technology-enhanced environment. **III. TEACHING, LEARNING, AND THE CURRICULUM.** Teachers: a. facilitate technology-enhanced experiences that address content standards and student technology standards.	NA
Assessment Examples Illustrated	**IV. ASSESSMENT AND EVALUATION.** Teachers: c. apply multiple methods of evaluation to determine students' appropriate use of technology resources for learning, communication, and productivity.	NA
Secondary Students Respond Positively	**II. PLANNING AND DESIGNING LEARNING ENVIRONMENTS AND EXPERIENCES.** Teachers: c. identify and locate technology resources and evaluate them for accuracy and suitability. **V. PRODUCTIVITY AND PROFESSIONAL PRACTICE.** Teachers: b. continually evaluate and reflect on professional practice to make informed decisions regarding the use of technology in support of student learning.	NA
PowerPoint Guides and Prompts Teaching	**VI. SOCIAL, ETHICAL, LEGAL, AND HUMAN ISSUES.** Teachers: b. apply technology resources to enable and empower learners with diverse backgrounds, characteristics, and abilities.	NA
Parent Pleased with Son's Opportunities	NA	NA

Clips	NETS-T	NETS-S
Tablet Computers Facilitate Learning; Students Discuss Tablet Use; Tablet Computers in Spanish	**I. TECHNOLOGY OPERATIONS AND CONCEPTS.** Teachers: b. demonstrate continual growth in technology knowledge and skills to stay abreast of current and emerging technologies. **II. PLANNING AND DESIGNING LEARNING ENVIRONMENTS AND EXPERIENCES.** Teachers: a. design developmentally appropriate learning opportunities that apply technology-enhanced instructional strategies to support the diverse needs of learners. d. plan for the management of technology resources within the context of learning activities. e. plan strategies to manage student learning in a technology-enhanced environment. **III. TEACHING, LEARNING, AND THE CURRICULUM.** Teachers: b. use technology to support learner-centered strategies that address the diverse needs of students. d. manage student learning activities in a technology-enhanced environment.	**3. Technology productivity tools** Students use technology tools to enhance learning, increase productivity, and promote creativity.

THEME 2: Software and Media

Technology is sometimes characterized in terms of hardware, software, and wetware. To benefit from any computer technology, a user must have access to a hardware device. The hardware device runs with compatible software which makes media such as text, sound, images, or video available to the user. For the technology to be useful, the user must engage with the hardware, software, and media by engaging his wetware, or brain. The students in the classrooms seen on the DVD have access to hardware including desktop computers, laptops, tablets, handheld devices, and peripheral devices. The students use the software and media on the devices as part of their learning activities. The choices of hardware, software, and media are important ones, and they influence the learning that results in the wetware. It is the learning that is the focus in these classrooms. As you watch the video clips that are listed and described below, you will interact with hardware and software that give you access to the video media, and you are encouraged to use your wetware to think about the relationship between the software and media and the student learning.

Below is a list of the eight clips related to Software and Media. Please watch these clips before considering the discussion and reflection questions that follow.

Laptops for Data in Fifth Grade.
Fifth graders in the classrooms of Amy Eisler and Shelly Couch at Cunningham Creek Elementary School in Jacksonville, Florida, use their laptops regularly to access information on the Internet and to work with software tools. These teachers think of their students' laptops as one of the essential learning tools in the classroom. Their students use the software tools alongside their textbooks, notebooks, and other materials. The teachers have developed strategies to help students manage their time and materials. Amy's students use a word processor to organize their genetics observations.

Quizdom System for Practice.
In Shelly Couch's fifth grade math class, students are held accountable for the learning they experience while using their laptop computers. A personal response system is one of the tools the students use to practice concepts and demonstrate their learning, and it feels more like a game than a test.

Challenger Center Provides Problem-Based Learning.
At the Challenger Learning Center in Jacksonville, sixth grade students are immersed in a simulation that places them in roles of NASA staff solving problems with a satellite. Students learn much more than science and geography through their experience.

Challenger Center Youth Leadership.
In a unique program, eighth grade students mentor sixth grade students in a simulated space station scenario at the Challenger Center. All of the students benefit from learning in new ways.

Geometer's Sketchpad for Inductive Reasoning.
Mike Patterson's goals include developing his students' geometry problem-solving skills. His high school students at Las Vegas' Advanced Technology Academy work through problems using classroom software. Mike uses geometric construction and modeling software to present concepts

and problems to students and for developing students' conceptual understanding. His students test conjectures that they develop with the software.

Benefits of Tablet Computers.

Elementary grades teachers at the Bolles School in Jacksonville, Florida, have begun using tablet computers in their classrooms for the full range of subject areas. A group of teachers describes the benefits their students have experienced since tablets were introduced into their classrooms. In these classrooms, the technology is used for student-centered learning.

Tablet Computers in Fourth Grade Science.

Students in Caryn Canfield's fourth grade class at the Bolles School in Jacksonville are learning social studies and developing their communications skills by researching, organizing, and creating presentations that they share with the class using the features of a tablet computer.

Tablet Computers in First Grade Mathematics.

In Jennifer Salley's first grade class at the Bolles School, each student creates a slide that demonstrates a subtraction example, and then the whole class practices as they watch all of the slides together.

Discussion Questions

1. In these classrooms, technology has been placed in the hands of first through twelfth grade students. Thinking about two of the classrooms, describe how student access to technology has caused these classrooms to operate differently from classrooms without technology. What is the same? What is different?

2. Each clip shows students using a specific software tool for learning. Notice the use of word processing, assessment systems, geometry software, and presentation software. Describe how three of the software tools support learning.

3. In addition to learning content area standards, what other learning is experienced by students in one of the technology-rich classrooms shown on the DVD? Can you identify specific content standards addressed in the classroom by referring to state or national standards for a content area? Many of the state and national standards are available at the Eisenhower National Clearinghouse website, http://www.enc.org/professional/standards/

4. Teachers establish rituals and routines with their students to help the learning process flow smoothly. For example, a middle school teacher may limit student movement to pencil sharpeners and rest rooms to specific times, and an elementary teacher may request that students use ink and cursive handwriting for final drafts of work. What routines do you observe in these classrooms that relate to the use of technology by students?

Reflection Questions

1. The students in these classrooms did not enter the classes knowing how to use the software they are using. What are a few methods a teacher might use to help students learn to use a new software tool?

2. In each clip, the teacher has high expectations of the students. The teacher believes that the students have the prior knowledge and skills to succeed with both the technology tasks and the learning that are presented in the classes. What do you believe is the role of teacher expectations in the technology-supported environment? What steps does the teacher take to increase the likelihood of student success?

National Educational Technology Standards for Students (NETS-S) Questions

1. NETS-S standard 2 is about social, ethical, and human issues. In the clips "Laptops for Data in Fifth Grade" and "Challenger Center Youth Leadership," students use technology in ways that gives them lifelong skills. For each of the clips mentioned, give an example of the students' use of technology that "supports lifelong learning, collaboration, personal pursuits, and productivity."

2. At the Challenger Learning Centers, students use technology to simulate complex real-world scenarios. As you watch the clip "Challenger Center Provides Problem-Based Learning," describe the type of real-world problems the students may be prepared to solve. Refer to NETS-S standard 6: Students employ technology in the development of strategies for solving problems in the real world.

National Educational Technology Standards for Teachers (NETS-T) and for Students (NETS-S) addressed in the clips:

Theme 2 DVD Clips: Software and Media	NETS-T	NETS-S
Laptops for Data in Fifth Grade	**VI. SOCIAL, ETHICAL, LEGAL, AND HUMAN ISSUES.** Teachers: a. model and teach legal and ethical practice related to technology use. d. promote safe and healthy use of technology resources. **II. PLANNING AND DESIGNING LEARNING ENVIRONMENTS AND EXPERIENCES.** Teachers: d. plan for the management of technology resources within the context of learning activities. e. plan strategies to manage student learning in a technology-enhanced environment. **III. TEACHING, LEARNING, AND THE CURRICULUM.** Teachers: a. facilitate technology-enhanced experiences that address content standards and student technology standards. d. manage student learning activities in a technology-enhanced environment.	**1. Basic operations and concepts** • Students demonstrate a sound understanding of the nature and operation of technology systems. • Students are proficient in the use of technology. **2. Social, ethical, and human issues** • Students practice responsible use of technology systems, information, and software. • Students develop positive attitudes toward technology uses that support lifelong learning, collaboration, personal pursuits, and productivity. **3. Technology productivity tools** • Students use technology tools to enhance learning, increase productivity, and promote creativity.
Quizdom System for Practice	**IV. ASSESSMENT AND EVALUATION.** Teachers: a. apply technology in assessing student learning of subject matter using a variety of assessment techniques. b. use technology resources to collect and analyze data, interpret results, and communicate findings to improve instructional practice and maximize student learning. c. apply multiple methods of evaluation to determine students' appropriate use of technology resources for learning, communication, and productivity.	**6. Technology problem-solving and decision-making tools** • Students use technology resources for solving problems and making informed decisions.
Challenger Center Provides Problem-Based Learning	**III. TEACHING, LEARNING, AND THE CURRICULUM.** Teachers: a. facilitate technology-enhanced experiences that address content standards and student technology standards. b. use technology to support learner-centered strategies that address the diverse needs of students. c. apply technology to develop students' higher order skills and creativity. d. manage student learning activities in a	**6. Technology problem-solving and decision-making tools** • Students use technology resources for solving problems and making informed decisions. • Students employ technology in the development of strategies for solving problems in the real world.

Theme 2 DVD Clips: Software and Media	NETS-T	NETS-S
	technology-enhanced environment.	
Challenger Center Youth Leadership	NA	**1. Basic operations and concepts** • Students demonstrate a sound understanding of the nature and operation of technology systems. • Students are proficient in the use of technology. **2. Social, ethical, and human issues** • Students practice responsible use of technology systems, information, and software. • Students develop positive attitudes toward technology uses that support lifelong learning, collaboration, personal pursuits, and productivity.
Geometer's Sketchpad for Inductive Reasoning	**III. TEACHING, LEARNING, AND THE CURRICULUM.** Teachers: a. facilitate technology-enhanced experiences that address content standards and student technology standards. b. use technology to support learner-centered strategies that address the diverse needs of students. c. apply technology to develop students' higher order skills and creativity. d. manage student learning activities in a technology-enhanced environment. **IV. ASSESSMENT AND EVALUATION.** Teachers: a. apply technology in assessing student learning of subject matter using a variety of assessment techniques.	**6. Technology problem-solving and decision-making tools** • Students use technology resources for solving problems and making informed decisions. • Students employ technology in the development of strategies for solving problems in the real world.
Benefits of Tablet Computers; Tablet Computers in Fourth Grade Science; Tablet Computers in First Grade Mathematics	**II. PLANNING AND DESIGNING LEARNING ENVIRONMENTS AND EXPERIENCES.** Teachers: a. design developmentally appropriate learning opportunities that apply technology-enhanced instructional strategies to support the diverse needs of learners. d. plan for the management of technology resources within the context of learning activities. e. plan strategies to manage student learning in a technology-enhanced environment. **III. TEACHING, LEARNING, AND THE CURRICULUM.** Teachers: a. facilitate technology-enhanced experiences that address content standards and student technology standards.	**3. Technology productivity tools** • Students use technology tools to enhance learning, increase productivity, and promote creativity. **4. Technology communications tools** • Students use a variety of media and formats to communicate information and ideas effectively to multiple audiences. **5. Technology research tools** • Students use technology to locate, evaluate, and collect information from a variety of sources.

Theme 2 DVD Clips: Software and Media	NETS-T	NETS-S
	c. use technology to support learner-centered strategies that address the diverse needs of students. d. apply technology to develop students' higher order skills and creativity. e. manage student learning activities in a technology-enhanced environment. **IV. ASSESSMENT AND EVALUATION.** Teachers: a. apply technology in assessing student learning of subject matter using a variety of assessment techniques. c. apply multiple methods of evaluation to determine students' appropriate use of technology resources for learning, communication, and productivity.	

THEME 3: The Internet and Virtual Schools

Today's classrooms fall on a continuum of Internet use, from online classes where the majority of interaction happens electronically, to a classroom without a computer where the Internet is used as an outside information source. Learning can be considered as a series of overlapping interactions between learners and other learners, between learners and instructors, and between learners and the subject matter. Any of these interactions may be mediated by technology, whether the learning happens inside or outside of a physical classroom. Different skills are needed for teaching that uses the Internet in a physical classroom than are needed for teaching in a virtual classroom. In the clips presented here, you'll enter the classrooms of teachers who have the skills to effectively use the Internet in their teaching.

Below is a list of the nine clips related to The Internet and Virtual Schools. Please watch these clips before considering the discussion and reflection questions that follow.

Online and Face-to-Face High School.
Elementary and secondary level students at the Odyssey Charter High School in Las Vegas, Nevada, have found a learning environment that meets their needs in a unique way. At the secondary level, students meet on campus with teachers one day each week, and they learn by using the multimedia and communications tools of the Internet for the remainder of the week.

Virtual School Advantages.
A group of Odyssey Charter High School students discuss why they have chosen online learning.

Learning Online.
Odyssey Charter High School students demonstrate how they complete their online course lessons and receive help in weekly classroom sessions.

Virtual School Teacher Skills.
Odyssey Charter High School teacher Robert Carter describes the qualities of an effective virtual school teacher.

Virtual English Course.
Middle and secondary students may never meet their teachers at the Florida Virtual School based in Orlando, Florida. However, the students have close relationships with each other and their teachers because they communicate daily via the Internet and phone. Each virtual school student has access to powerful and flexible online learning tools. In this clip, English teacher Heidi Allen shows the tools and methods her students use for learning.

Virtual Geometry Course.
Florida Virtual School geometry teacher April Schmidt demonstrates how her students learn mathematics online.

Virtual School Philosophy.

The Florida Virtual School is based on mastery learning at "any time, any place, and any pace." Ms. Allen and Ms. Schmidt discuss the school's course design philosophy and their ideas about the future of education.

Scholarly Writings Online Engage Students.

World history is a series of stories, and Valarie Young's high school students at the Advanced Technology Academy explore some of the classic stories through the writing of prominent archeologists. The students use articles in online journals to analyze events from multiple perspectives as they prepare to discuss their viewpoints in a class roundtable.

EZ Geometry Website Supports Student Work.

High school math teacher Mike Patterson created his website to extend his ability to help his students learn at the Advanced Technology Academy of Las Vegas. The site has become a comprehensive resource for his students, their parents, and other teachers.

Discussion Questions

1. The Internet is used for several purposes by the teachers in these clips. Discuss one purpose for using the Internet for learning in each classroom featured in the clips. Then, discuss the reasons the teachers or students have for choosing to use the Internet as a tool for learning.

2. Students learning in public virtual schools are expected to meet the same academic standards as students in traditional public schools, but the methods used for teaching and learning are different. How is the virtual school experience shown in the two virtual schools on the DVD different from your classroom experience for students and for teachers?

Reflection Questions

1. One comment that is sometimes heard about the teaching profession is that it can be isolating. How can the Internet be used to reduce a teacher's professional isolation?

2. One of the benefits of using the Internet for teaching is its potential to involve parents in the learning process. Describe a way that a teacher can use the Internet to increase a parent's involvement in the student's education.

National Educational Technology Standards for Students (NETS-S) Questions

1. The students at Odyssey Charter High School and their families have chosen a virtual school because they value the benefits of learning online. Characteristics of online learning have caused the students to "develop positive attitudes toward technology uses," as stated in the NETS-S standard 2. Listen to the students in the following clips and list three factors that contribute to their positive attitudes toward educational technology: Online and Face-to-Face High School, Virtual School Advantages, and Learning Online.

2. The NETS-S standards encourage student use of four types of technology tools: productivity tools as described in standard 3, communications tools as described in standard 4, research tools as described in standard 5, and problem-solving and decision-making tools as described in standard 6. Listen to the teachers from the Florida Virtual School in the following clips, and list the tools used in their classes that fit each of four standards: Virtual English Course, Virtual Geometry Course, and Virtual School Philosophy.

3. At the Advanced Technology Academy, teachers use Internet resources in very different ways to meet the needs of students in their content areas. As you watch "Scholarly Writings Online Engage Students" and "EZ Geometry Website Supports Student Work," compare and contrast the purposes served in the two classes by Internet materials, by referring to NETS-S standards 5 and 6.

National Educational Technology Standards for Teachers (NETS-T) and for Students (NETS-S) addressed in the clips:

Theme 3 DVD Clips: The Internet and Virtual Schools	NETS-T	NETS-S
Online and Face-to-Face High School; Virtual School Advantages; Learning Online; Virtual School Teacher Skills; Virtual English Course; Virtual Geometry Course; Virtual School Philosophy	**III. TEACHING, LEARNING, AND THE CURRICULUM.** Teachers: a. facilitate technology-enhanced experiences that address content standards and student technology standards. b. use technology to support learner-centered strategies that address the diverse needs of students. c. apply technology to develop students' higher order skills and creativity. d. manage student learning activities in a technology-enhanced environment. **IV. ASSESSMENT AND EVALUATION.** Teachers: a. apply technology in assessing student learning of subject matter using a variety of assessment techniques. b. use technology resources to collect and analyze data, interpret results, and communicate findings to improve instructional practice and maximize student learning. c. apply multiple methods of evaluation to determine students' appropriate use of technology resources for learning, communication, and productivity. **VI. SOCIAL, ETHICAL, LEGAL, AND HUMAN ISSUES.** Teachers: b. apply technology resources to enable and	**1. Basic operations and concepts** • Students demonstrate a sound understanding of the nature and operation of technology systems. • Students are proficient in the use of technology. **2. Social, ethical, and human issues** • Students develop positive attitudes toward technology uses that support lifelong learning, collaboration, personal pursuits, and productivity. **3. Technology productivity tools** • Students use technology tools to enhance learning, increase productivity, and promote creativity. **4. Technology communications tools** • Students use telecommunications to collaborate, publish, and interact with peers, experts, and other audiences. • Students use a variety of media and formats to communicate information and ideas effectively to multiple audiences. **5. Technology research tools** • Students use technology to locate, evaluate, and collect information from a variety of sources.

Theme 3 DVD Clips: The Internet and Virtual Schools	NETS-T	NETS-S
	empower learners with diverse backgrounds, characteristics, and abilities. identify and use technology resources that affirm diversity d. facilitate equitable access to technology resources for all students.	
Scholarly Writings Online Engage Students	III. a, b, c, d. IV. a, b, c. VI. b, d.	**5. Technology research tools** • Students use technology to locate, evaluate, and collect information from a variety of sources.
EZ Geometry Website Supports Student Work	III. a, b, c, d. IV. a, b, c. VI. b, d.	**6. Technology problem-solving and decision-making tools** • Students use technology resources for solving problems and making informed decisions.

THEME 4: Technology across the Curriculum

Each content area makes its own set of demands on learners in terms of the levels of communication, data, and information literacies that are required. One of the main advantages of technology for learning is its flexibility and adaptability. Often the same hardware and software can be used in a wide range of grade levels, skills, and content areas. Teachers in each content area have capitalized on the relative advantages of the available technology to solve the educational problems they encounter. In this section of the DVD you will see eight teachers teaching different subjects to students with different needs and abilities using different combinations of technology. In each case, the students are succeeding.

Below is a list of the seven clips related to Technology across the Curriculum. Please watch these clips before considering the discussion and reflection questions that follow.

Presentation Software in Literature.
In Patty Kmieciak's high school English class at the Bolles School in Jacksonville, Florida, students check their knowledge of literature by using a presentation that is designed after a game show model. After testing their knowledge by answering questions, students create questions for their peers.

Communication System for Foreign Language.
Kate Pritchard's middle school German students at Episcopal High School of Jacksonville have more time to practice their reading and speaking because of the school's language lab. Headphones and microphones reduce interference as students communicate with partners, and the teacher can participate in any conversation. Students use computers to record and analyze their own speech. The school has recognized the effect of interference on student learning in other classes, and has installed audio enhancement systems in classrooms to increase student attention.

Graphing Calculators in Trigonometry.
In Mike Patterson's trigonometry class at the Advanced Technology Academy in Las Vegas, students test various changes in an equation to see the effects on the graph of the equation. They share their graphs with the class using the overhead projector and calculator display.

Tablet Computers in World History.
Don Page has replaced overhead transparencies, chalkboards, and maps with his tablet computer. Using *Journal* software, he displays maps and documents for the class, and uses the tablet's stylus to illustrate discussions of events in his world history class at the Bolles School in Jacksonville.

Website and *Photoshop* in Photography.
Richard Chamberlain's photography students at Episcopal High School of Jacksonville attended a gallery show to learn the techniques of a prominent photographer. In their classroom, they study the photographs using the gallery website, and then they practice the techniques using image manipulation software.

Composition Software and MIDI in Music.

Students in Lynn Howard's music theory course at Episcopal High School of Jacksonville use music composition software to simultaneously see and hear the notes as they work. Creating and playing music gives the students hands-on practice with the music concepts.

SmartBoards for Hearing Impaired Students.

Colette Cook teaches a group of middle school students who are deaf or hard of hearing and who have other special needs, and Teresa Smith teaches a class of hearing impaired elementary school students at the Florida School for the Deaf and Blind in St. Augustine, Florida. They both use _SmartBoards_ with their classroom computers to give their students hands-on experience in language development.

Discussion Questions

1. Choose three of the classrooms from this theme and discuss the following:
   - An educational problem that was addressed with technology,
   - The technology that was used, and
   - The relative advantage offered by the technology over using a non-technology approach to the problem.

2. Imagine that you are a teacher in two of the classrooms in this theme. Think about the following:
   - What would you say to the parents of your students to help them understand how you use technology in your class?
   - What would you say to visiting members of the school board?

Reflection Questions

1. When a teacher is planning a technology-supported lesson, what factors do you think need to be considered in the lesson's preparation?

2. What are three ways you can learn about the advantages of technology for students in a specific grade level of content area?

National Educational Technology Standards for Students (NETS-S) Questions

1. In the Episcopal High School language lab, students learn a foreign language through intensive practice with feedback. Discuss how this use of technology meets both NETS-S standards 3 and 4.

2. The trigonometry students in Mike Patterson's class use graphing calculators for individual practice, small group discussion, and in large group discussion of problems. Refer to NETS-S standard 6 to discuss the types of real-world problem-solving skills the students in this class are developing, both in mathematics and in other areas of learning.

National Educational Technology Standards for Teachers (NETS-T) and for Students (NETS-S) addressed in the clips:

Theme 4 DVD Clips: Technology Across the Curriculum	NETS-T	NETS-S
Presentation Software in Literature	**III. TEACHING, LEARNING, AND THE CURRICULUM.** Teachers: a. facilitate technology-enhanced experiences that address content standards and student technology standards. d. manage student learning activities in a technology-enhanced environment.	NA
Communication System for Foreign Language	**IV. ASSESSMENT AND EVALUATION.** Teachers: a. apply technology in assessing student learning of subject matter using a variety of assessment techniques. b. use technology resources to collect and analyze data, interpret results, and communicate findings to improve instructional practice and maximize student learning. c. apply multiple methods of evaluation to determine students' appropriate use of technology resources for learning, communication, and productivity.	**4. Technology communications tools** <ul><li>Students use telecommunications to collaborate, publish, and interact with peers, experts, and other audiences.</li></ul>
Graphing Calculators in Trigonometry	**II. PLANNING AND DESIGNING LEARNING ENVIRONMENTS AND EXPERIENCES.** Teachers: a. design developmentally appropriate learning opportunities that apply technology-enhanced instructional strategies to support the diverse needs of learners. d. plan for the management of technology resources within the context of learning activities. e. plan strategies to manage student learning in a technology-enhanced environment. **III. TEACHING, LEARNING, AND THE CURRICULUM.** Teachers: a. facilitate technology-enhanced experiences that address content standards and student technology standards. b. use technology to support learner-centered strategies that address the diverse needs of students. c. apply technology to develop students'	**6. Technology problem-solving and decision-making tools** <ul><li>Students use technology resources for solving problems and making informed decisions.</li></ul>

Theme 4 DVD Clips: Technology Across the Curriculum	NETS-T	NETS-S
	higher order skills and creativity. d. manage student learning activities in a technology-enhanced environment.	
Tablet Computers in World History	**II. PLANNING AND DESIGNING LEARNING ENVIRONMENTS AND EXPERIENCES.** Teachers: a. design developmentally appropriate learning opportunities that apply technology-enhanced instructional strategies to support the diverse needs of learners. d. plan for the management of technology resources within the context of learning activities. **III. TEACHING, LEARNING, AND THE CURRICULUM.** Teachers: a. facilitate technology-enhanced experiences that address content standards and student technology standards.	NA
Website and *Photoshop* in Photography; Composition Software and MIDI in Music	**II. PLANNING AND DESIGNING LEARNING ENVIRONMENTS AND EXPERIENCES.** Teachers: a. design developmentally appropriate learning opportunities that apply technology-enhanced instructional strategies to support the diverse needs of learners. d. plan for the management of technology resources within the context of learning activities. e. plan strategies to manage student learning in a technology-enhanced environment. **III. TEACHING, LEARNING, AND THE CURRICULUM.** Teachers: a. facilitate technology-enhanced experiences that address content standards and student technology standards. b. use technology to support learner-centered strategies that address the diverse needs of students. c. apply technology to develop students' higher order skills and creativity. d. manage student learning activities in a technology-enhanced environment.	**3. Technology productivity tools** • Students use technology tools to enhance learning, increase productivity, and promote creativity.
SmartBoards for Hearing Impaired Students	**VI. SOCIAL, ETHICAL, LEGAL, AND HUMAN ISSUES.** Teachers: b. apply technology resources to enable and empower learners with diverse backgrounds, characteristics, and abilities.	**4. Technology communications tools** • Students use telecommunications to collaborate, publish, and interact with peers, experts, and other audiences. • Students use a variety of media and formats to communicate information

Theme 4 DVD Clips: Technology Across the Curriculum	NETS-T	NETS-S
	c. identify and use technology resources that affirm diversity e. facilitate equitable access to technology resources for all students.	and ideas effectively to multiple audiences.

CHAPTER 2
GETTING TO KNOW THE STUDENTS IN TODAY'S SCHOOLS

This chapter will help you to:
- Distinguish the characteristics of today's students
- Describe the national priorities in educational technology and 21st century skills
- Identify the six categories of the National Educational Technology Standards for Students (NETS-S)

National Educational Technology Standards for Teachers (NETS-T) addressed in this chapter:
V. PRODUCTIVITY AND PROFESSIONAL PRACTICE.
Teachers use technology to enhance their productivity and professional practice. Teachers:
- Use technology resources to engage in ongoing professional development and lifelong learning.
- Continually evaluate and reflect on professional practice to make informed decisions regarding the use of technology in support of student learning.
VI. SOCIAL, ETHICAL, LEGAL, AND HUMAN ISSUES.
Teachers understand the social, ethical, legal, and human issues surrounding the use of technology in PK-12 schools and apply those principles in practice. Teachers:
- Apply technology resources to enable and empower learners with diverse backgrounds, characteristics, and abilities.

Interactive Reading Strategies included in this chapter:
- 📖 Venn Diagram
- 📖 Double Entry Journal

THE MILLENNIAL GENERATION

Advances in computer technology over the last generation have changed the way we work and live.

	Industrial Age	Information Age
Work	work was product-oriented	work is knowledge-oriented
Workers and skills	workers were knowers with limited skill sets to complete repeated tasks	workers are learners needing flexible, advanced skill sets for rapid innovation
Time and authority	a central authority prescribed tasks to be done in discrete time periods	workgroups identify and solve problems over extended time periods, then communicate results

National Educational Technology Standards for Students (NETS-S) Question
To what extent do you think the NETS-S guide students in development of Information Age abilities? Give specific examples from the NETS-S for each category of Information Age abilities shown in the table above.

Technology has also changed the way children learn. Children born after 1982 have been called the Millennial Generation because they attended school in 2000 and after. They are considered a distinct group because they have experienced digital technology throughout their lives. These children embrace interactive media that make them curious, self-reliant, and adaptable. They prefer interactive rather than broadcast media. Interactive learning is active and learner-centered. Children can learn independently of adults, and they become fluent in non-text media and are expert information navigators. Children are adept at assembling information to create a new product, and they are accustomed to a social, situated, and concrete learning experience.

Technology has even changed the way we think. Learning causes long-term changes in the physical structure of the brain as neural pathways in the cognitive functioning area are developed through adolescence (Bransford et al., 1999). The quality and amount of information acquired is reflected in brain structure. Short-term changes in the brain occur as regions of the brain are activated during cognitive stimulation. Different regions of the brain are activated when a person is hearing, seeing, and speaking. The brain is most active when a person is encountering something for the first time, and is generating thoughts during engagement in a task (Rose & Dalton, 2002). Children who grow up with interactive multimedia have brains that work well with these tools.

In addition, technology has changed student expectations of education. Children recognize the differences between school and the world, and they live in an era of choice. They and their families are savvy consumers of media and education options. If they rely on technology and expect access to technology to enrich their learning, it is increasingly likely that if they do not find technology used in their schools, they will look for a school that satisfies their needs. To see what some children said about the importance of technology in their lives, see the article "What Children Think about Computers" from the *Children and Computer Technology* journal at http://www.futureofchildren.org.

Interactive reading strategy

You can use the Venn diagram template on page 23, or use the Venn diagram template in *Inspiration* software, or use the online Venn diagram builder at http://www.readwritethink.org/student_mat/index.asp

Individual: Create a Venn diagram comparing yourself and your own experience with technology to a millennial child and his or her experience with technology. How are you like a millennial child and how are you different? How will you adapt your teaching for millennial children in your classroom?

Group: Compare your Venn diagram with others, and compile a list of adaptations for teaching millennial students. How is your diagram different from the diagrams of others? What causes the differences among individuals?

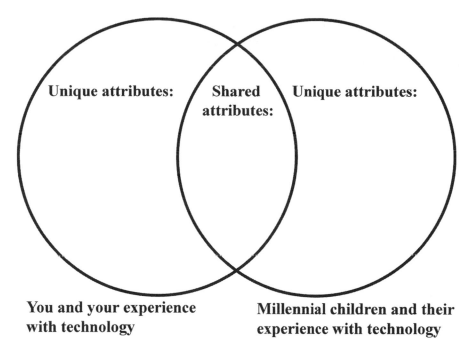

Unique attributes: **Shared attributes:**   **Unique attributes:**

You and your experience with technology   **Millennial children and their experience with technology**

Children are interested in learning. When learning to play games, children show that they are interested learning to do something themselves, doing it well, and sometimes doing it better than someone else—they interact with themselves, with information, and with others. They think about learning.

The changes in technology and how children learn have implications for education. Educators know that learning happens best when the learner is willing. Children learn best by taking on meaningful, authentic tasks. The role of the teacher has shifted to being more of a mentor, model, and guide. In the student-centered classroom, students assume more responsibility for their education. Applying computers to traditional education systems restricts the potential of the technology. This happens because computers did not exist when schools were designed, and it is difficult to envision a radical change in education structure that best uses the strengths of technology. To serve today's students, effective classrooms adopt attributes of Information Age workplaces:

- knowledge orientation
- flexibility
- advanced skills
- problem solving
- long-term projects
- communication of results

Technology tools can transform learning in the Information Age. We want our schools to be places where *why* is more important than *how*. Technology must offer a way for students to think, present, research, and do, in different, more enriched, and more powerful ways. We want our students to understand ways that technology helps them learn and adapt. The main long-term competitive skill is skill at learning. It is the cognitive skills, such as learning how to learn and adapt, that will be most valuable in education, work, and life. We recognize that 90% of the technology we will be using in ten years either has not yet been invented, or isn't accessible now, and the majority of the job opportunities that today's kindergarteners will have don't exist now. We are preparing students for a world we cannot envision. Therefore, students need to become expert learners and they need skills in information and technology fluency. Technology-rich classrooms are most successful when advanced technologies are linked with advanced teaching strategies.

Technology supports learning when students:
- Learn by doing and receive feedback on their learning
- Refine their understanding and build knowledge
- Visualize complex or abstract concepts
- Model real-life situations
- Interact with information or people

Technology supports learning when it is used in an environment in which:
- People identify problems and solve them in a real-world context
- Students interact with practitioners
- Students explore and test ideas
- Students increase their abilities and interest

Computers empower students when:
- Students pose and pursue questions
- Learning is recognizable and enjoyable
- Learning is challenging and interesting
- Long-term sustained effort is needed for complex tasks
- Learning is self-directed and exploratory
- Results, evidence, or products of learning are shared

How well we teach students to work and live within the information environment will help determine whether future generations fully participate in social, political, and cultural life, or remain passive spectators. The ***Clips from the Classroom*** DVD will show you examples of technology used by teachers to teach millennial students in supportive and empowering ways. If you are interested in more information about millennial students, you can visit the *Millennials Rising* site at millennialsrising.com, or read *Students in Today's Schools* at the National Education Technology Plan site at nationaledtechplan.org.

Clips from the Classroom DVD Activity 2.1: Millennial Students

- Select two of the clips listed below to watch while thinking about millennial students. What approaches does the teacher in the clip use to effectively teach Information Age students to be expert learners in the content area?

  Clips for this question:
  THEME: Transforming Teaching and Learning
  - Secondary Students Respond Positively
  THEME: Software and Media
  - Laptops for Data in Fifth Grade
  THEME: The Internet and Virtual Schools
  - E-Z Geometry Website Supports Student Work

THE NATIONAL EDUCATIONAL TECHNOLOGY PLAN AND 21ST CENTURY SKILLS

School has many functions today. If we asked the founders of this nation what schools are for, we would hear that our schools were established to develop the citizens of a young democracy. Democracies require citizens prepared for self-governance. Literacy is not enough. It takes critical inquiry and skills of evaluation, among a great many other abilities and inclinations. School is the only place with the specific role of developing citizens. This role is an important one, because democracies do not come with guarantees, and they do not endure without committed citizens.

Teachers in a democratic society develop students' abilities to live a good life and to achieve their dreams, and they also prepare students for participation in society. When we ask leaders of business and industry what schools are for, they tell us about the need for knowledge workers in the new economy, the need to educate people to be workers and consumers so we will be competitive, and that education should be reformed to advance the role of the United States in the global economy.

Our strength as a nation is important, and testable abilities matter. If we recognize that education has several essential purposes, then educators have important responsibilities in preparing students for an unknowable future. The "21st Century Skills" serve as one guide for preparing student, for their many roles in life. These skills were developed by a group of education, business, and government leaders working to address the range of education needs and challenges of work and life in the 21st century. They have been integrated into the National Education Technology Plan. The National Education Technology Plan for the U.S. Department of Education was developed in 2004 as part of a long-range guide for using technology effectively to improve student academic achievement. The plan establishes a national strategy supporting the effective use of technology to improve student academic achievement and prepare them for the 21st century. The plan was designed with the attitudes, beliefs, and assumptions of today's students in mind, and it was created with broad input from thousands of education stakeholders. It emphasizes selected initiatives, including the use of technology to improve student assessment and school accountability, elearning to reach all students with challenging appropriate education, and broadband access to powerful communication and information resources. The plan is located at http://www.nationaledtechplan.org/

The 21st century skills are grouped into the following areas:

1. Digital-Age Literacy
   - Basic, scientific, economic, and technological literacies
   - Visual and information literacies
   - Multicultural literacy and global awareness

2. Inventive Thinking
   - Adaptability and managing complexity
   - Self-direction
   - Curiosity, creativity, and risk taking
   - Higher-order thinking and sound reasoning

3. Effective Communication
- Teaming, collaboration, and interpersonal skills
- Personal, social, and civic responsibility
- Interactive communication

4. High Productivity
- Prioritizing, planning, and managing for results
- Effective use of real-world tools
- Ability to produce relevant, high-quality products

Go to http://www.21stcenturyskills.org/

National Educational Technology Standards for Students (NETS-S) Question

Look at the list of 21st century skills above. Many of them are not specifically technology skills, but the development of the skill can be supported and enhanced with technology. Select three of the skills from the list that are not technology skills, describe a way that technology could be used to develop the skill, and identify the NETS-S standard that would apply to the use of technology that you suggest.

These are complex skills designed to meet the complex challenges of preparing millennial students to succeed in the unknowable future and to govern a nation. What technologies will help students reach these goals? Many tools are thinking and planning tools, also called mindtools. If you haven't seen these tools in the hands of children, you may wonder whether they will work in our schools. While watching the **Clips from the Classroom** DVD, you will see students in such schools at work with technology.

Clips from the Classroom DVD Activity 2.2: 21st Century Skills
- Watch two of the clips listed below while considering the 21st century skills.
- Make note of the skills students are learning in the class.
- Describe the role of technology in helping the students learn these skills.

Clips for this question:
THEME: Software and Media
- Laptops for Data in Fifth Grade
- Challenger Center Provides Problem-Based Learning
- Challenger Center Youth Leadership
- Tablet Computers in Fourth Grade Science
- Tablet Computers in First Grade Mathematics

THEME: The Internet and Virtual Schools
- Online and Face-to-Face High School
- Learning Online
- Virtual English Course
- Virtual Geometry Course
- Virtual School Philosophy

Interactive reading strategy

You can use the Double Entry Journal template below, or the example from
http://www.readwritethink.org/lessons/lesson_view.asp?id=228

Individual: Create a Double Entry Journal with a column for the 21st century skills, and a column for examples. List an example for each skill from your life or from a career. How could an elementary teacher teach one of the skills? A secondary teacher?

Group: Compare journals. For which skills was it most difficult to list examples? Which skills are most appropriate for elementary students, and which for secondary students?

Topic: 21st Century Skills

Double Entry Journal

Direct quote from 21st Century Skills	Example of the skill in action

THE NATIONAL EDUCATIONAL TECHNOLOGY STANDARDS

The 21st century skills serve as a guide to the type of learning required by today's students, and the national and state subject area standards offer guidelines to the content knowledge recommended for students. The teacher works to ensure that students acquire the content knowledge and the thinking skills, while developing abilities to use technology. The International Society for Technology in Education (ISTE) has developed the National Educational Technology Standards for Students (NETS-S) as a guide for the appropriate use of technology for teaching and learning. The

NETS for students (NETS-S) have been followed by NETS for teachers and administrators (NETS-T), as guides for developing the skills with technology that are most important today. Each chapter in this guide is associated with the NETS for teachers that are addressed by the chapter materials and activities. All of the NETS are located at http://cnets.iste.org/students/s_stands.html

CHAPTER 3
EFFECTIVE TECHNOLOGY FOR TODAY'S STUDENTS

This chapter will help you to:
- Identify the practices in technology integration that have been shown in research to be effective for supporting and enhancing student learning
- List the cautions about the use of technology in education
- Describe approaches for evaluating the effects of technology for particular educational needs

National Educational Technology Standards for Teachers (NETS-T) addressed in this chapter:
II. PLANNING AND DESIGNING LEARNING ENVIRONMENTS AND EXPERIENCES.
Teachers plan and design effective learning environments and experiences supported by technology.
Teachers:
- Apply current research on teaching and learning with technology when planning learning environments and experiences.
- Identify and locate technology resources and evaluate them for accuracy and suitability.
III. TEACHING, LEARNING, AND THE CURRICULUM.
Teachers implement curriculum plans that include methods and strategies for applying technology to maximize student learning. Teachers:
- Apply technology to develop students' higher order skills and creativity.

Interactive Reading Strategies included in this chapter:
- 📖 Inverted Triangle Strategy
- 📖 Point—Counterpoint—Endpoint

WHAT WORKS: RESEARCH-BASED PRACTICE

As long as technology has existed in education, it has been studied, evaluated, and criticized. Parents, legislators, educators, and taxpayers make reasonable demands when they ask what learning benefits children receive from using classroom technology.

Your knowledge of recent findings on technology effectiveness will serve you in several ways:
- Planning instruction for your students using appropriate technology
- Ensuring that your students successfully achieve the state and national technology standards
- Communicating to parents the importance of technology in your classroom
- Working with administrators to acquire the best technology for your students
- Writing successful grants to enhance your students' technology access
- Leading and mentoring so children in other classrooms will have technology-using teachers
- Demonstrating the technology knowledge and skills you will need for professional advancement along the career ladder and for National Board Certification

One goal of education is to prepare students for success in the roles they may take on throughout life. This goal assumes an essential connection between what children experience in school and what they experience in life. The boundaries between classrooms and the world blend when children engage in complex real-world issues. The technology they use for learning is effective when children are able to use the raw materials of the Information Age to develop higher-order thinking skills and communicate ideas and solutions to a wide audience. The higher-order thinking skills are those skills found higher on Bloom's taxonomy, and they include evaluation, analysis, and synthesis.

There are examples from all content areas of students using information in complex ways with technology, just as adults and professionals use information in life. Mathematics students use population simulation software and population data to report findings to governments on the impact of growth on services. Government students learn the judicial system by creating a legal case brief online and publishing it online. Journalism students collaborate on "ezines." Technology tools that support student development of high-level thinking skills are cognitive mapping software such as *Inspiration*; simulation software such as *MicroWorlds*, the *Sim* programs, or *Amazon Trail*; WebQuests and online journeys; online projects such as GLOBE; online access to experts and practitioners; and e-mail, chat, and conferencing applications.

Clips from the Classroom DVD Activity 3.1: Higher-Order Thinking Skills

In Mike Patterson's high school geometry class, students use *Geometer's Sketchpad* software to work with the complexities of the concepts in an inquiry-oriented hands-on experience. As you watch his students in the video clip "*Geometer's Sketchpad* for Inductive Reasoning," list the higher-order thinking skills the students are developing. You can read more about higher-order thinking skills at the North Central Regional Educational Laboratory (NCREL) EnGauge website, http://www.ncrel.org/engauge/skills/invent6.htm

A great many technology-using educators can tell the stories of their students for whom technology has made a positive difference. These stories inspire and inform the practice of other teachers.

Clips from the Classroom DVD Activity 3.2: What Works with Technology

In each of the clips listed below, a teacher is using technology to make positive differences for students. As you watch the three clips, identify what is working well for the students in the class because of the technology they are using.

Clips for this question:
THEME: Transforming Teaching and Learning
- Student Achievement Increases
- Tablet Computers Facilitate Learning
THEME: Technology across the Curriculum
- Website and *Photoshop* in Photography

In education, we need to add to the stories and case studies with scientifically based experimental evidence in order to know with greater certainty that the students, subjects, and technology in our classrooms are well matched, and that we are transforming learning to the fullest extent possible.

Several recent, major studies and reviews of the research have documented the positive effects of educational technology on student achievement. Wenglinsky (1998) found that higher mathematics scores were related to access to computer technology in conjunction with teachers who had been educated in technology use and the use of computers to learn new, higher-order concepts. Lou, Abrami, and d'Apollonia (2001) found that small group learning had significantly more positive effects than individual learning on student individual achievement. Other recent meta-analyses in technology have found positive effects for interactive distance education for K-12 students (Cavanaugh, 2001), computer-assisted instruction in science education (Bayraktar, 2001-2002), and computer-based instructional simulation, especially hybrid simulations that mix traditional expository presentation with simulations (Lee, 1999). A synthesis of research of computer-assisted instruction on student achievement in science (Christmann & Badgett, 1999) showed that students receiving traditional instruction accompanied by computer-assisted instruction experienced higher academic achievement than those receiving only traditional instruction, and an analysis of the uses of educational software (Murphy et al., 2002) found a positive association between student achievement and the use of educational software products to support instruction in reading and math. The recent meta-analysis of student learning across grades, content areas, and technology applications conducted by Waxman, Lin, and Michko (2003) consolidated research to determine that teaching and learning with technology has a small, positive effect on students' cognitive outcomes when compared to traditional instruction. Further, the results did not differ significantly among student, school, teaching and technology characteristics.

The body of literature on specific uses of technology for learning is extensive and has been built over decades. It should be used to guide educators in choosing effective technology to meet learning needs. Educators shown on the ***Clips from the Classroom*** DVD have learned their technology strategies as a result of experience, professional wisdom, sharing viewpoints with colleagues, and familiarity with the education research on technology for learning. You will find from watching them in their classrooms and hearing their comments that there are times when they choose not to use technology.

Clips from the Classroom DVD Activity 3.3: Advantages of Technology

In Valarie Young's high school world history class, technology is used for some learning activities. The technology is one of a bright palette of resources that students use. As you watch the clip "Assessment Examples Illustrated," consider and do the following:

- Compare the activities that happen with technology and those that happen without technology.
- What are the reasons Valarie might have for choosing the technology-supported activities and the non-technology-supported activities?

Interactive reading strategy

You can use the Inverted Triangle template below or design your own.

Individual: Complete the Inverted Triangle Diagram to lead you through steps in selecting a technology-centered solution for a specific learning problem. You may need to access other sources of information as you think through a learning need and explore possible solutions. Identify the **NETS-S standards** that apply to the solution you propose.

Group: Locate someone working on a problem similar to yours, and share solutions. How do the age of the students, the academic content area, or the cognitive demand of the subject influence the range of possible technology solutions to the learning problems?

Topic: Choosing eduational technology for teaching

Inverted Triangle Strategy

At the top of the triangle, write a learning problem you wish to consider. For example, reading comprehension or math problem solving. Complete the next levels of the triangle. Continue this way until you have a specific technology application to address the problem.

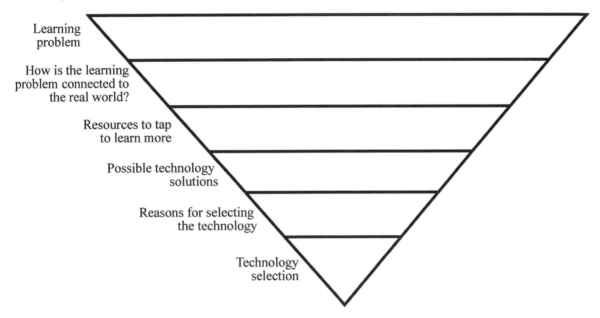

Experienced technology-using educators have reasons for choosing the technology they use, and for choosing when and how to use technology in their instructional designs. The following section outlines cautions for the use of technology for K-12 learning.

A BALANCED VIEW: APPROPRIATE USES OF TECHNOLOGY

As with any learning resource, there are situations in which technology is the most appropriate choice, and other situations in which other resources are more appropriate. In large measure, education is about guiding students to learn to use a wide range of tools and resources, to evaluate the tools and resources in light of their needs, and to independently select those that will meet their needs. Students need help in learning to use new tools, and in achieving balance in their choices. While extensive evidence supports the use of technology for many learning problems, technology represents only one band in the problem-solving palette. Educators need information on the reasons to balance the use of technology with other tools in order to be equipped to make the best decisions.

Advocates for limiting the use of technology by children cite the following cautions:
- Technology may be a substitute for physical activity, which children need for their long-term health.
- Technology may replace interpersonal communication if children are using computers in isolation or if they are not using the communication capabilities of the computers.
- Children risk repetitive stress injury if they are not taught to change their body position or if they use the computer for extended periods of time without breaks.
- Students do not need expensive computers to access information if they attend schools with well-equipped and adequately staffed libraries.
- Students using the Internet need to learn ethical and social responsibility.
- Computer use may diminish a student's experience in creative endeavors and community activities.

Research has shown how technology, used in developmentally appropriate ways, leads to gains in learning. The following guidelines can be used to optimize the benefits of technology for student learning.
- Technology is most effective when **integrated with curriculum and assessment**. In a review of studies, the CEO Forum (2001) stated that "technology can have the greatest impact when integrated into the curriculum to achieve clear, measurable educational objectives."
- Technology applications that **enable student collaboration** tend to lead to improved achievement. Working with partners in the classroom or communicating with peers at a distance can lead to learning benefits when technology is used. In an analysis of studies on Integrated Learning Systems (ILS), Kulik (2003) concluded that an ILS appears to be more effective when students work in pairs on lessons (p. 25).
- Technology increases learning when it provides **prompts, feedback, and assessments** to the student and teacher about student performance or progress in learning (Kulik, 2003).
- Technology is most effective when it is used as **part of the regular activities** in the classroom (Kulik, 2003).
- Technology can aid students in developing higher-order thinking skills when students **know the process of problem solving and have opportunities to use technology in problem solving** (Wenglinsky, 1998).
- Technology can aid students in developing critical thinking skills when students **use technology tools to integrate text and images and then present an explanation** (Mayer, 2001).

In each of the following clips, technology is used in appropriate ways to support the students in their content and skill development. Watch the three clips below, and list the examples of appropriate technology use, making reference to the points outlined above.

Clips for this question:
THEME: Software and Media
  ☉ *Quizdom* System for Practice
THEME: Technology across the Curriculum
    ☉ Composition Software and MIDI in Music
    ☉ *SmartBoards* for Hearing Impaired Students

Interactive Reading Strategy

You can use the Point—Counterpoint—Endpoint template below, or you can create your own.

Individual: Imagine that a parent, school board member, or community member expressed to you one of the cautions about computer use listed on page 33 of this guide (Point). Write a fact-based response that addresses the concern (Counterpoint). Develop a plan or compromise that satisfies both the Point and Counterpoint positions (Endpoint). Include a **NETS-S standard** that applies to the plan you propose.

Group: With a partner, choose a caution about the use of technology for learning (Point). As an individual, develop a fact-based response (Counterpoint). Share your response with your partner, and then join another pair to jointly develop plans or compromises (Endpoints) to your Point-Counterpoint positions.

Point: a cautious viewpoint about the use of technology in education	**Counterpoint:** a fact-based response to the viewpoint	**Endpoint:** a plan or compromise that satisfies both positions

EVALUATING THE EFFECTS OF TECHNOLOGY FOR LEARNING

Once a teacher selects and implements a technology-supported learning experience with students, how can the effects of the experience be evaluated? Teachers are by nature reflective, having developed the ability to constantly conduct status checks as lesson are progressing, and then making a series of adjustments to improve the outcome for students. Teachers adopt a process of reflective practice, a systematic method for thinking back over a completed lesson and making mental notes about changes to include the next time the lesson is taught. Sometimes this reflection is formalized through the use of note cards, lesson plan annotations, or voice and video recordings. Teachers have begun to take the next step in reflecting on and evaluating the success of their classroom practice: action research to measure the effects of their methods on student outcomes.

Action research is the process of systematically evaluating the consequences of educational decisions and adjusting practice to maximize effectiveness (McLean, 1995). The process is situation-specific, cyclical, and ongoing, with the results from one cycle leading to further action research. "As action researchers, teachers take action and effect positive educational change in the specific school environment that was studied...with the goals of gaining insight, developing reflective practice, effecting positive changes in the school environment (and on educational practices in general), and improving student outcomes and the lives of those involved" (Mills, 2003, pp. 5-6).

Developing proficiency in action research supports:
- strategic problem solving for specific educational challenges;
- positive communication between administrators and teachers;
- empowerment of teachers and administrators;
- increased professional satisfaction;
- flexible, solution-oriented thinking;
- increased professional motivation to improve practice;
- increased collegiality, ongoing inquiry, self-reflection, and decision-making skills;
- increased expectations for student learning;
- increased expectations for self-improvement.

In the case of technology, a teacher may use an action research plan to collect information in the process of judging the effects of technology, such as the use of electronic books to help learning disabled students increase their interest in reading and their use of reading strategies, concept mapping software to improve abstract concept development in physical science, or publishing an online writing "ezine" to improve interest and experience in writing.

The central ideas in action research begin with the teacher as the focal person in his or her research. The teacher asks a real question about a real issue, and hopes to move toward a solution. The teacher starts from his or her current place in teaching and tries to bring about some improvement (McNiff, Lomax, & Whitehead, 2003).

According to Osterman and Kottkamp (1993), educators have many reasons for engaging in action research. Everyone needs professional growth opportunities, and all professionals want to improve. All professionals can learn and are capable of assuming responsibility for their own professional growth and development. People need and want information about their own performance. Collaboration enriches professional development (p. 46).

Action Research Action Steps (adapted from Mills, 2003):
1. State a research question.
2. Locate and summarize findings in literature related to the research question.
3. Recommend a teaching action informed by the literature findings and targeted at the question.
4. Identify the individuals who will be responsible for the action.
5. Identify the individuals who will be consulted or informed.

6. Identify the individuals who will collect data on student progress.
7. Plot a projected timeline for the action steps, data collection, and data analysis.
8. Identify the resources needed to carry out the plan.
9. Identify support and encouragement network.
10. Be sure that the research question involves teaching and learning, is within the teacher's locus of control, is an issue the teacher feels passionate about, and is something the teacher wants to change or improve.
11. Describe the situation that will be changed or improved, and the critical factors that affect the situation.
12. Hypothesize how the critical factors affect the situation, and how the situation can be changed or improved.
13. Collect data on the current status of the situation.
14. Enact the plan.
15. Collect data to evaluate the effectiveness of the plan.
16. Analyze the data.
17. Summarize the meaning of the data.
18. Identify opportunities to share the knowledge with other educators, such as through a professional conference or journal, or through a school or district website.
19. Consider a new cycle of action research with a refined research questions.

Technology offers teachers unprecedented choices in instructional materials, access to an enormous repertoire of strategies and lessons, and a vast array of tools for reflecting on and improving learning outcomes.

The teachers shown on the ***Clips from the Classroom*** DVD are professionals who have weighed the options available to them and selected technology that works in their classrooms. They reflect and evaluate their decisions and aim for ongoing improvement in student learning.

Clips from the Classroom DVD Activity 3.5: Reflective Teaching
> All of the clips in the "Transforming Teaching and Learning" and "Software and Media" themes of the DVD show teachers who reflect on the decisions they have made about the technology they use in their classrooms. As you watch **two video clips from each theme**, consider and do the following:
> - Identify the teacher's goals and priorities regarding technology use in his or her class.
> - Why does the teacher use the technology?
> - What changes has the teacher made in his or her use of technology?

The next chapter describes how teachers keep up with the changes in educational technology and how they plan, organize, and manage technology in their classrooms.

CHAPTER 4
PLANNING FOR TECHNOLOGY IN TEACHING AND LEARNING

This chapter will help you to:

- Describe characteristics of effective educator professional development activities and examples of professional development experiences for learning to use educational technology.
- List steps in designing and assessing technology-supported learning.
- Identify procedures for organizing and managing classroom technology.

National Educational Technology Standards for Teachers (NETS-T) addressed in this chapter:

II. PLANNING AND DESIGNING LEARNING ENVIRONMENTS AND EXPERIENCES.

Teachers plan and design effective learning environments and experiences supported by technology. Teachers:

- Apply current research on teaching and learning with technology when planning learning environments and experiences.
- Plan for the management of technology resources within the context of learning activities.
- Plan strategies to manage student learning in a technology-enhanced environment.

III. TEACHING, LEARNING, AND THE CURRICULUM.

Teachers implement curriculum plans that include methods and strategies for applying technology to maximize student learning. Teachers:

- Facilitate technology-enhanced experiences that address content standards and student technology standards.
- Use technology to support learner-centered strategies that address the diverse needs of students.
- Apply technology to develop students' higher order skills and creativity.
- Manage student learning activities in a technology-enhanced environment.

IV. ASSESSMENT AND EVALUATION.

Teachers apply technology to facilitate a variety of effective assessment and evaluation strategies. Teachers:

- Apply multiple methods of evaluation to determine students' appropriate use of technology resources for learning, communication, and productivity.

V. PRODUCTIVITY AND PROFESSIONAL PRACTICE.

Teachers use technology to enhance their productivity and professional practice. Teachers:

- Continually evaluate and reflect on professional practice to make informed decisions regarding the use of technology in support of student learning.

VI. SOCIAL, ETHICAL, LEGAL, AND HUMAN ISSUES.

Teachers understand the social, ethical, legal, and human issues surrounding the use of technology in PK-12 schools and apply those principles in practice. Teachers:

- Promote safe and healthy use of technology resources.

Interactive Reading Strategies included in this chapter:
- 📖 Spider Map
- 📖 Ten Most Important Words
- 📖 Think—Pair—Share
- 📖 Design a Job Aid

The diagram below shows stages in designing instruction that uses technology, adapted from Roblyer (2006). You read in Chapter 3 of this activity guide about solving education problems with technology and about using action research to evaluate the implementation of the solution, so you are familiar with two of the stages. In this chapter you will read about preparing yourself to use technology, planning instruction by beginning with the assessment of learning, and how to organize and manage classroom technology.

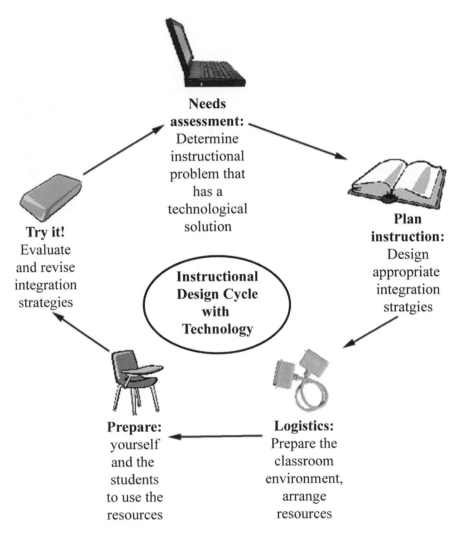

Needs assessment: Determine instructional problem that has a technological solution

Plan instruction: Design appropriate integration stratgies

Instructional Design Cycle with Technology

Try it! Evaluate and revise integration strategies

Logistics: Prepare the classroom environment, arrange resources

Prepare: yourself and the students to use the resources

Clips from the Classroom DVD Activity 4.1: Designing Instruction

Think about the stages of designing technology-enhanced instruction while you watch Patty Kmieciak and her high school English class reviewing Shakespeare in the "Technology across the Curriculum" video clip called "Presentation Software in Literature." Record an example of what Patty did in her design for each stage below:

1. Determine instructional problem that has a technological solution—
2. Design appropriate integration strategies—
3. Prepare the classroom and arrange resources—
4. Prepare self and students to use the resources—

PROFESSIONAL DEVELOPMENT FOR TECHNOLOGY-USING EDUCATORS

Studies carried out by the U.S. Department of Education show that 20-25% of teachers feel well prepared and integrate technology into teaching and 88% of teachers indicated that professional development activities prepared them to some extent to use technology (2001). In this era of growing knowledge, technological change, and education reform, teachers have a responsibility to be lifelong learners. Professional development programs are organized experiences that teachers use to stay updated in their fields. "The extent to which teachers are given time and access to pertinent training to use computers to support learning plays a major role in determining whether or not technology has a positive impact on achievement" (Valdez et al., 2000).

Effective professional development programs for educators share several features. They are tailored to the needs of adult learners, they are responsive to the professional demands of teachers, and they make a positive difference in the work of teachers. Adult learners have characteristics that distinguish them from younger learners. Adults need to choose from various options that fit their preferences, interests, and styles. Teacher learning should focus on an important end goal: student learning. Adults place importance on confidence, comfort, calm and competence, and generally do not enjoy risk or surprise. Adults sustain their learning in teams or support groups, and they take the time needed to integrate new learning into their practice.

Professional development in the use of technology for teaching is unique because it crosses grade levels and content areas. In addition, each teacher has a different set of technology abilities and feelings toward learning to use technology. Five stages of technology adoption have been identified, and they have varying labels, as shown in the following table.

Stages of technology adoption

Concerns Based Adoption Model, Hord et al., 1987	Apple Computer (ACOT), 1995	Nisan-Nelson, 2001
Non-use and orientation	Entry	Familiarization
Preparation and routine	Adoption	Utilization
Refinement	Adaptation	Integration
Integration	Appropriation	Reorientation
Renewal	Invention	Evolution

Not only do technology adopters move through a series of stages as they change their uses of technology, but late adopters are very different from early adopters. Late adopters want proof of results before spending time and money. Late adopters want a complete and finished product or plan. Early adopters enjoy using technology while it is somewhat unproven and they can participate in the testing and debugging of applications.

Interactive reading strategy

You can use the Spider Map template below, or you can use the template at the Enchanted Learning site, http://www.education-world.com/tools_templates/index.shtml#graphicOrganizers

<u>Individual</u>: In the center of the Spider Map, write the name of the stage where you feel you currently fit for technology adoption. On the legs of the spider, list the reasons why you placed yourself at that stage.

<u>Group</u>: With a partner or small group, list strategies you could use to move to the next stage. Try discussing your strategies with someone else who is at the stage as you are, and then see if a person at the stage above you has other ideas.

Spider Map for Stages of Technology Adoption:

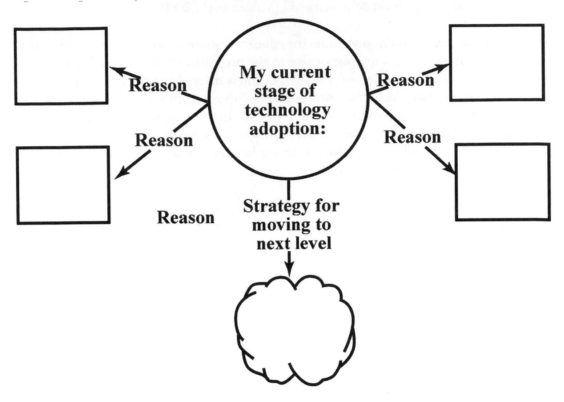

Effective professional development programs are sensitive to the differences among technology users and make adjustments for individual abilities and preferences. These programs have a clear purpose related to student outcomes, and they offer choices in the schedule and style of activities. Several types of professional development programs fit these criteria. Many are ongoing and can be teacher-initiated. A few types are described here.

1. A **learning community** is a group of learners collaboratively studying a theme or body of knowledge unified by a common area of interest or career goal. Teachers who belong to a learning community may teach at the same school, or may join together from different schools. A learning community may use meetings or electronic communication to collaborate.
- After School Online, http://www.tappedin.org
- Classroom Connect Connected Teacher, http://www.classroom.com/community/community.jhtml
- Education World, http://www.education-world.com/a_curr/
- Teachervision, http://www.teachervision.fen.com/

2. Joining **professional associations** is a way to meet other educators, read articles about current practice, and participate in conferences with colleagues. In addition to reading and writing for journals and attending and presenting at conferences, teachers are encouraged to apply for awards sponsored by many professional groups. Each of these activities has its own rewards. Each school subject area has a professional association. For educators with an interest in educational technology, many states have educational technology associations. The national educational technology group in the United States is the International Society for Technology in Education (ISTE).

- ISTE, http://www.iste.org

3. **Grantseeking** is an activity that directly enhances a teacher's classroom resources. Developing a grant project for education can be a long-term commitment. It requires careful thought and planning, but it offers unmatched opportunities to learn in the process. Many grant proposals include information about the school's mission and the students served, the needs of the community, and an identified learning need. The grant project proposes to meet the need using an approach that is likely to succeed, based on similar efforts; meets established standards such as content area standards or NETS-S standards; and requests funding to accomplish the project. The proposal lists methods that will be used to document the success of the project, and the qualifications of the individuals who will be responsible for carrying out the project. Many organizations, both public and private, exist to financially support education projects of all sizes. Below are a few sources for locating funds for class and school technology projects.

- ISTE's Funding Resources, http://www.iste.org/resources/funding/index.cfm
- Education World Grants Center, http://www.education-world.com/grants/
- Technology and Learning Grants, http://www.techlearning.com/grants.html

4. Busy teachers have discovered the benefits of **online courses and workshops** to help them acquire new skills and knowledge. Most local colleges and universities offer online courses, and some offer entire degree programs online. For teachers looking for short-term learning experiences, several organizations offer online short courses and workshops. Online learning can be a chance to make contact with colleagues who are too distant to meet in person. Whether a teacher elects to devote days or years to an online learning program, he or she should ensure that certain prerequisites are met. An online learner needs regular access to a dependable, Internet-connected computer, and time and space to focus on the course activities. Online learning requires independence and motivation, as well as strong skills in reading, writing, organizing, and using the computer. The sites listed here offer technology-related online learning for teachers.

- Apple Learning Interchange, http://ali.apple.com
- Connected University, http://cu.classroom.com/info.asp
- Skylight, http://www.skylightedu.com
- Teacher Universe, http://www.riverdeep.net/teacheruniverse/
- THE Institute, http://www.thejournal.com/institute
- ISTE NETS Online, http://www.netsonline.iste.org/

5. Access to **onsite workshops and classes** is limited by a teacher's geographic region and ability to travel. Most schools and districts host workshops on topics needed by teachers, and most colleges and universities offer continuing education classes and graduate degrees for inservice teachers. Regional centers supported by state and other education agencies offer professional development

activities, and there are often classes offered at conferences. Classes and workshops can be places to make contact with other teachers and to expand the professional network.

6. A **mentor** is a guide, a confidante, and a tutor. Mentors guide mentees in making transitions into new roles, in learning new skills, and in staying motivated to persevere when conditions become challenging. Mentor relationships are sometimes assigned and defined for an identified purpose and timeframe, while others are organically formed as needed. Both the mentor and mentee grow in their roles as they learn together. The sites listed here have background information on mentoring.

- Teacher Mentors, http://www.teachermentors.com/
- Mentoring Leadership and Resource Network, http://www.mentors.net
- Mentoring, from the George Lucas Education Foundation, http://glef.org/educators.html
- National Mentoring Partnership, http://www.mentoring.org/index.adp

7. When following the **Authentic Task Approach** to professional development, a group of teachers meets with a facilitator to work together to accomplish a task that they define. A task may be to develop lessons that integrate existing technology in more powerful ways, or to create a research-based guide that addresses a real learning problem. The product should always be something that will be used to improve outcomes for students.

- ATA steps, http://www.serve.org/sunray/atamodel.htm
- ATA in Depth, http://www.enc.org/professional/guide/learn/ata/depth/

8. **Lesson study** is a systematic process by which groups of teachers seek to improve their practice by planning, teaching, observing, critiquing, and refining lessons. The benefits include both the refined lesson and the deeper understanding of good teaching that results from the collaborative process. The sites listed here provide more information.

- Lesson Study Research Group, http://www.teacherscollege.edu/lessonstudy/
- National Science Foundation Lesson Study Communities Project, http://www2.edc.org/lessonstudy/
- Research for Better Schools' "What is Lesson Study?", http://www.rbs.org/currents/0502/what_is_lesson_study.shtml

9. **Examining student work**, also called **looking at student work**, is an approach to reflection that focuses on student learning. While looking together at samples of student work, teachers consider questions about teaching and learning, including the degree to which student standards are met. These teachers believe that students' work in schools is serious work, and that it offers keys about the functioning of the school. The sites listed here provide more details.

- Looking at Student Work, http://www.lasw.org/index.html
- What Story Does the Work Tell?, http://www.philaedfund.org/slcweb/index.htm
- Looking Collaboratively at Student Work, http://www.essentialschools.org
- Examining Student Work, http://www.enc.org/professional/guide/strategies/work/

Clips from the Classroom DVD Activity 4.2: Professional Development

High school history teacher Valarie Young elaborates on her professional development experiences that have led to her success as a technology-using educator. In the video clip from the theme "Transforming Teaching and Learning" called "Technology Improves

Teaching Skills," she describes both formal and informal methods she used in her professional development. As you watch the clip, consider and do the following:

- List the learning strategies that have worked for her.
- What strategies do you think would work for you, if you designed your own technology professional development plan?
- Why?

DESIGNING TECHNOLOGY-ENHANCED LEARNING EXPERIENCES

Planning to use technology in teaching and learning requires a teacher to merge his or her knowledge of students, the content, the technology, and good teaching practice to make the most effective choices. An instructional plan begins with the end point: the learning goal. The goals of a unit of instruction include the broad goals of education, the content area and technology standards, and 21st century skills. In any lesson, the events of instruction are to some extent determined by the teacher's guiding philosophy of teaching.

The **directed learning** philosophy assumes that learners respond in predictable ways to events, including reward and punishment, and that learning is based on information processing, storage, and retrieval. Technology in a directed-type classroom is often used to remediate gaps or weaknesses, to develop recall or performance, to accelerate motivated students, to provide individualized instruction, and to help students work more efficiently. The **constructivist learning** philosophy assumes that learners must be motivated to learn, and that learning happens best when prior knowledge is activated and integrated in a social context. In the constructivist classroom, technology is often used to encourage creativity, to aid metacognition, to increase application of knowledge for problem-solving, to support group work, to develop technical and visual literacy. A **merged** philosophy assumes that part of what learners need to learn (about 30%) is knowledge best acquired through directed methods, and the rest (about 70%) is employment or application of knowledge developed with constructivist approaches (adapted from Roblyer, 2006).

Clips from the Classroom DVD Activity 4.3: Teaching Philosophy

Geometry teacher Mike Patterson uses technology in different ways for different learning goals. Watch him in the "Software and Media" video clip called "*Geometer's Sketchpad* for Inductive Reasoning." Mike follows a merged philosophy, using technology in both directed and constructivist ways. Think about this clip while you consider and do the following:

- Give an example of when Mike uses technology in directed learning activities.
- Give an example of when Mike uses technology in constructivist learning activities.
- How does he assess student learning?
- How are the **NETS-S** addressed differently when each philosophy is prominent?

43

Assessment

Each philosophy values a different kind of learning, and requires a different approach to assessment. Assessments of learning may be designed to measure students' content knowledge, skill, or ability to use technology. To design an effective assessment:

1. Determine the most important outcome of learning.
2. Focus student attention on the desired outcomes. The learning may be demonstrated using a process, a product, or both. Technology can play a role in many demonstrations of learning.
3. Create an assessment experience that will ensure that you get clear evidence of the outcome.
4. Develop an appropriate scoring system for the assessment that reflects both the goals and the students' current development al stage.

Assessments take several forms. Formative assessments evaluate learning at specific checkpoints, and they are used optimally for continuous feedback. They allow opportunities for students to revise work as they go and to collaborate with peers and others. Summative assessments that serve to evaluate learning at an endpoint should be aligned with standards and should be used after students have had enough opportunities to practice the skills that will be assessed. Self-assessments teach students to evaluate their own performance, which is a step in becoming an independent lifelong learner. Performance-based assessments include portfolios, projects, presentations, writing, and demonstrating. They are generally used to give students experience with an authentic activity that requires higher-level skills such as application, synthesis, and evaluation.

Clips from the Classroom DVD Activity 4.4: Assessment of Learning

Because Valarie Young teaches with a variety of activities in her history class, she employs a variety of assessment methods to check student learning. Watch the video clip in "Transforming Teaching and Learning" called "Assessment Examples Illustrated."

- List the assessment methods Valarie uses.
- Which assessment methods are formative?
- Which assessment methods are summative?
- Which methods give students practice with real-world skills?
- Which methods require higher-level thinking skills?

The assessment method influences teaching and learning. When student learning is assessed using authentic, open-ended instruments, then teaching and learning become authentic and inquiry-based. **Rubrics** are especially well suited to assessing complex and creative student activity. A rubric is a set of scales for rating complex performance and providing detailed information to improve performance. Effective rubrics include all important elements of a task listed as simple steps, use distinct and descriptive ratings covering a range of performance levels, and communicate performance clearly. Rubrics can be developed by the teacher or jointly with students. Students often use them as guides during learning, and parents refer to them for information on what is expected of students.

To develop a rubric for learning with technology, refer to these steps:
1. Begin with the learning objective. Determine the target outcomes.

2. Identify the cognitive and performance evidence that can be used to determine success for each outcome.
3. List the indicators required for successful performance of each outcome.
4. Determine weighting factors and provide an equation students can fill in to calculate a score.
5. Arrange the information on a page in table form.
6. Use the rubric for an evaluation of a presentation or activity.
7. Revise the rubric as necessary.
8. Guide your students in designing their own rubric for a project!

The completed rubric or assessment plan can guide the rest of the planning process. The lesson's outcomes or objectives should be matched to technology applications and activities that extend the students' abilities or enable to them to learn better, more deeply, or more quickly. From here, the lesson planning process involves creating instructions for activities that will guide students to success with the goal. Students may need "think sheets" that include strategies for integration of information from multiple sources, organization of time and materials, and elaboration of ideas in order to achieve the goal of the lesson.

During the lesson, use the five elements of effective instruction (Morrison & Lowther, 2005):

1. Introduce activities, their importance, and prior knowledge and skills needed for success.
2. Provide necessary information and instructions for information obtained by students.
3. Provide activities for applying and practicing with information and skills.
4. Build in ways for students to get a variety of feedback and to reflect on their learning.
5. Structure a culminating activity that consolidates learning.

The next section of the chapter will provide guidelines for planning the activities in which students will engage with and without technology.

Interactive reading strategy
You can use the Ten Most Important Words template below, or you can create your own.

Individual: Think about the ten words you feel are most important for someone to know about organizing and managing technology in a classroom. List the words with a reason for each word.

Group: Use the Think—Pair—Share discussion strategy. First, think about the ten words you feel are most important for someone to know about organizing and managing technology in a classroom. Next, pair with a partner and compare your lists of words. Agree on the most important word. Then share your number one word and your reasons with another pair or the whole group.

Ten Most Important Words about organizing and managing classroom technology:

The 10 most important words, listed before reading the next section	Reasons for choosing the words	Changes in the list after reading the next section
1		
2		
3		
4		
5		
6		
7		
8		
9		
10		

ORGANIZING AND MANAGING TECHNOLOGY

The technology-using educator is able to provide the most valuable technology-supported learning experiences to students when both the students and the technology are working to their fullest potential. This section outlines ways to help students work in safe and healthy ways with technology, and ways to organize the physical and instructional aspects of the classroom for the benefit of students.

Safety
Above all, students must work safely. To reduce exposure to electromagnetic radiation from computer monitors, switch to LCD panels or a projector. Position monitors so users can sit at least two to three feet away from the screen and from surrounding monitors and TVs. Computer tables should be at least 30 inches deep. Table height should allow students to use chairs that let their feet touch the floor, see the monitor at eye level, and use the keyboard at a comfortable height. The mouse should not be located so far to the side of the keyboard that students have to reach sideways—the upper arm should still hang down near the body to avoid shoulder and back strain. To reduce wrist injury, students should take short breaks, switch jobs, support their wrists, stretch, and vary their activity. Wireless keyboards and mice also help to alleviate stress because they allow greater flexibility in positioning. Lighting should be subdued and localized to reduce eyestrain and glare. People work best with noise-absorbing rooms, neutral colored walls, nonreflective surfaces, adjustable furniture, at least three feet between computers, and space for movement.

Classroom procedures and arrangements
Managing the technology-enabled classroom means establishing procedures for use of time, hardware and software, data, and space. Classrooms in which technology is used seamlessly have a culture that supports student independence. In these classrooms, students help each other to solve problems with the technology and with learning. Students and teachers view learning and the work they produce as public and sharable. They support the progress of others, in and out of the classroom. They are able to work harmoniously in close proximity.

Cultures of technology learning function in classrooms with one computer and in classrooms with thirty-one computers. The difference is in the time students are able to spend actively using a computer. In one-computer classrooms, the computer is often used as a presentation station by the teachers and by groups of students. Student groups are often allocated equal amounts of time on a rotation schedule to complete small group projects or to contribute to a class project. For example, each group may make an entry into a class database of countries or authors, or each group may add a slide to a presentation. Group work can be streamlined through the use of templates for files or documents that students will create. With access to more computers, student projects can be more extensive. To increase the students' on-task work, create interesting problems for them to solve and build in chances for them to make decisions about their learning. The table below compares the advantages and disadvantages of different numbers of students using classroom computers.

The number of students using a computer	Advantages	Disadvantages
One	The computer is used in a way best suited to the individual; each student must develop the skills.	Each student gets little time on the computer.
Two or three	Students interact during the process and learning generally increases.	Be cautious of dominant students. Not all software works well for groups.
Small group	Students can take roles in a simulation or a cooperative assignment.	Tasks must be planned carefully, space must be adequate, and software must support group use.
Large group	Components of a large project can be delegated to subgroups.	The computer functions as a tool to support a broader task. Work must be carefully planned.
Whole class	Demonstrations or presentations can be made with individuals controlling the computer.	Display and sound must be adequate for whole class.

Clips from the Classroom DVD Activity 4.5: Student Grouping

In four of the classrooms on the DVD, teachers alternate between large groups of student using a computer and individual students or pairs using a computer. The decision about the optimal student-to-computer ratio is made based on the abilities of the students, the nature of the content and skills, and practical constraints of time and other resources.

In the classrooms of Valarie Young, Mike Patterson, Shelly Couch, and Amy Eisler, students move among different technology configurations. In the "Software and Media" video clip called "*Geometer's Sketchpad* for Inductive Reasoning," Mike Patterson's students engage in activities that occur with the whole class using a computer in presentation mode as a focus of discussion and in activities that use individuals at computers for project work. Consider and do the following:

- Contrast the kinds of activities done in each arrangement with benefits of using the computers in each arrangement.
- Note the benefits of using a single computer for whole-class interaction in a class such as the Spanish class seen in the "Transforming Teaching and Learning" clip called "Tablet Computers in Spanish."

- Discuss the degree to which **NETS-S standards** are achieved in the different arrangements.

To assist students who need help with the technology, a team of student coaches can be designated to take turns being on call. Posters can outline common steps used on the computers, and quick references sheets or binders with instructions can be placed near each computer. Savvy students enjoy creating these sheets for the class to help with upcoming projects. Students will need instructions for using removable disks, network file storage space, software, printers, Internet sites, and additional hardware such as cameras or scanners. Students may need guidance regarding acceptable use policies or working with the Internet filter. The teacher needs to establish and enforce computer rules about when it is appropriate to use the computer, what the computer may be used to do, and what files may be accessed.

Managing time and resources

To help technology-supported lessons flow smoothly, the teacher should establish procedures for managing technology resources. Original software should be copied and stored in a safe place in the event the computer fails. All classroom files and software should be descriptively named and disks clearly marked. Printer supplies should be kept handy, and students should be encouraged to print only the pages they need. Student and teacher work files should be backed up to CDs or the network. Students should be taught proper treatment of keyboard, monitor, cables, mouse, and disks. Students and parents need to become familiar with safe online behavior and steps to follow when something uncomfortable or inappropriate is found online.

Time management practices contribute to smooth lessons with technology. Teachers can institute a help signal and a group attention signal, along with clear procedures for ending computer time. For example, a poster with student names on clothespins can indicate whether a student has "Been there" or "Not yet." Red cups on the desk or monitor top can mean help needed, and a blue cup can mean a cool thing has been accomplished or discovered. The following table lists methods for controlling student use of computers.

Paradigms of Computer Use (Geisert & Futrell, 1995)

Milestone	Specific events in a computer program are used to determine how long a session should be.	Appropriate for tutorial or practice software.
Timed	Each student or group uses the computer for an assigned time period.	Quicker students will learn more than slower students.
Task-defined	Students or teams are assigned tasks to complete, such as a publication or project.	Focus is on a product.
Open time/As needed	Students use the computer when they need to, up to a set time limit.	Requires a strict system or monitoring, used when the computer is a reference.

Interactive reading strategy

Design a job aid that students could use as a reference to help them with a technology task. The job aid can be a quick reference sheet or a poster for common tasks. You can design the steps as a list, as a web, as a timeline, or using one of the tools at http://www.readwritethink.org/student_mat/index.asp. Include a title and step-by-step guidelines for a computer procedure using age-appropriate language.

As you watch the teachers on the ***Clips from the Classroom*** DVD, you may not notice at first the classroom management techniques they employ when their students use technology. These teachers established rituals and routines early in the school year, and their students learned and use them almost without thought.

Clips from the Classroom DVD Activity 4.6: Classroom Management

In elementary and secondary classrooms on the DVD, the teachers use appropriate routines to streamline the work of the students. As you watch the classrooms listed below, list the techniques used by teachers and students for effective and efficient learning.

- **Transforming Teaching and Learning Theme:** "Technology Manages Flow of Activities." In this video clip, history teacher Valarie Young focuses on the transitions among the activities in her lessons.
- **Software and Media Theme:** "Laptops for Data in Fifth Grade." Here Amy Eisler and Shelly Couch demonstrate management strategies in their fifth grade laptop classrooms.
- **Technology across the Curriculum Theme:** "Graphing Calculators in Trigonometry." Mike Patterson's trigonometry students use high- and low-technology tools during the stages of learning to graph equations.

CHAPTER 5
EXPANDING THE CLASSROOM WITH TECHNOLOGY

This chapter will help you to:
- Describe the digital divide and its implications for students and educators.
- List examples of classroom activities that are enhanced through the use of technology to access outside resources and foster communication between students and a variety of audiences.

National Educational Technology Standards for Teachers (NETS-T) addressed in this chapter:
V. PRODUCTIVITY AND PROFESSIONAL PRACTICE.
Teachers use technology to enhance their productivity and professional practice. Teachers:
- Use technology to communicate and collaborate with peers, parents, and the larger community in order to nurture student learning.
VI. SOCIAL, ETHICAL, LEGAL, AND HUMAN ISSUES.
Teachers understand the social, ethical, legal, and human issues surrounding the use of technology in PK-12 schools and apply those principles in practice. Teachers:
- Apply technology resources to enable and empower learners with diverse backgrounds, characteristics, and abilities.
- Identify and use technology resources that affirm diversity
- Facilitate equitable access to technology resources for all students.

Interactive Reading Strategy included in this chapter:
📖 Fishbone Diagram

THE DIGITAL DIVIDE

How well we teach children to cope with the information environment will help determine whether future generations fully participate in social, political, and cultural life, or remain passive spectators. Whether we take steps to ensure that all students have access to the information and the skills to use the information will in part determine who participates.

Information archives take many forms: the human mind, carvings, paintings, paper, analog recording, and digital storage. For as long as knowledge has been generated and stored by humans as information, inequities have limited access to the information. The inequities may result from geographic barriers, language barriers, financial barriers, or political barriers. Our society has worked to remove those barriers in the effort to open the access to information democratically. Still, access to digital information is limited by one's access to digital devices, ability to use the devices, and skills at using the information. It is these aspects of access that define the digital divide.

The **digital divide** is a difference in access to digital information among groups of people. In schools, the difference may be a result of gender, ethnicity, socioeconomic status, disability, or teacher expectations and philosophy. Each of these factors will be explored here.

Gender

Boys are more interested and involved in technology than girls, generally speaking. They state that they are more involved in technology than other interests, and they spend more time using technology than girls do. Tapping into this user group, software manufacturers and websites tend to reflect more typically male interests and reward systems, thus the popularity of action and military computer games. This divide in the recreational use of technology appears to span age groups. In high school, an indicator of serious interest in technology is enrollment in the Advanced Placement Computer Science course. Only 15 percent of students taking the AP computer science exam in 2001 were girls (*Education Week*, 2001). If fewer girls study computer science in high school, it seems likely that fewer would study it at the college level, limiting their careers in this important and growing field. The U.S. Department of Education reported that in 1998 women received 27% of undergraduate degrees in computer science, down from a high of 37% in 1984—a gender divide in technology education that is contributing to a shortage of skilled technology workers (Gehring, 2001).

Ethnicity

Access to computers both at home and at school has led to a divide along ethnic lines. White students are twice as likely to have access to home computers as black students. Students in schools with predominantly minority enrollments are more likely to use technology for drill, practice, and test-taking skills. In contrast, white students in more affluent communities are creating websites and multimedia presentations (*Education Week*, 2001b), giving them an edge in developing their 21st century skills.

Socioeconomic status

A student's family income and community resources influence his or her access to technology. Only 22% of children in homes with incomes less than $20,000 per year had access to a home computer, compared with 91% of those from homes with incomes over $75,000. When low-income children have access to computers at home, they use them less than in high-income homes (Becker, 2000). Despite similar school-level access, 63 percent of teachers in schools with the lowest enrollment of poor students (less than 11 percent of students eligible for free or reduced-price lunch) reported that they used computers or the Internet for instruction during class time, while 47 percent of teachers in schools with 50 to 70 percent of students eligible reported this use (NCES, 2002). If a student lacks access to technology at home, the school must fill the gap, but many students have no access to technology at home or at school.

Disability

A majority of schools and classrooms serve students with special needs, whether or not the need has been formally identified and documented. Each year 6 million U.S. students receive special education services (U.S. Department of Education, 2004). For these students technology can mean the difference between learning on grade level and falling behind. However, according to U.S. Department of Commerce reports, more than twice as many disabled people as nondisabled people had never used a computer in 2002 (NCES, 2002).

Teacher expectations and philosophy

Teachers tend to integrate technology least with low achieving students even when they are the group most likely to benefit. Teachers with the most constructivist teaching philosophies are stronger users of computers: They use computers more frequently, they use them in more challenging ways, they use them more themselves, and they have greater technical expertise (Becker, 2000, p. 16).

Several factors appear to influence the use of computers in school, and all of the factors widen the access divide for the students who can least afford a disadvantage. The implications for the differential treatment among groups of students regarding technology access in schools include students who are learning differently in their classrooms and at home, students who develop fewer technical job skills, and students who have limited access to information that could improve their learning or their quality of life.

Teachers cannot control all of the factors that contribute to the digital divide among students, but several solutions are within a teacher's sphere of influence. Examples of these solutions are shown in the following list.

- Choose classroom software and websites to reflect diversity of backgrounds and perspectives.
- Support and design websites that are universally accessible to all users, regardless of ability or disability.
- Work for equitable funding, technical assistance, and professional development for schools by communicating with administrators, school board members, and legislators about your concerns.
- Find technology that may be hidden in schools. Equipment may have been purchased for a discontinued program or a teacher who has left.
- Find budgets that allow technology purchases, such as Title I, ESOL, ESE, career, vocational, library, PTO, or foundation accounts and grants. Keep a wish list ready for end-of-year purchases, and keep in touch with the individuals who make purchasing decisions.
- Look for people with funds who need ideas, including community organizations and business partners.
- Look for groups with equipment to hand down. Government agencies, businesses, civic groups, and colleges have surplus equipment on a regular basis.
- Keep old computers going, because they can be used for low-intensity applications such as reference or word processing.
- Encourage technology-avoiding students to use technology to do something they like.
- Help develop technology after school, extended day, or club programs for underserved groups of students, and consider involving their families.
- Bring diverse technology-using role models to students using pictures, video, conferences, and guest appearances.
- Seek technology professional development opportunities to increase your skills, and encourage a colleague or team to join you.

Interactive reading strategy

You can use the Fishbone Diagram shown on page 53, or use the templates from Enchanted Learning located at http://www.enchantedlearning.com/graphicorganizers/fishbone/

Individual: Create a Fishbone Diagram using the digital divide as the result, and factors contributing to the divide as causes. Include details about each factor.

<u>Group</u>: Add factors or details to a group Fishbone Diagram based on your experiences and your knowledge of schools in your community.

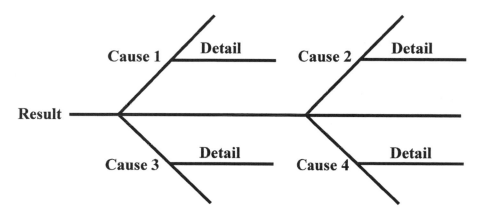

BRINGING THE WORLD INTO THE CLASSROOM AND THE CLASSROOM TO THE WORLD

Educators have long sought ways to add relevance to student learning, and to increase community and parent involvement in education. Today, technology gives parents, businesses, organizations, and governments an opportunity to become more involved in education, and it gives students a channel for participating in authentic community activities.

Communication technology

Communications technologies (including email, chat, discussion boards, mailing lists, blogs, and conferencing) all offer low-cost, short-term methods for teachers to communicate with parents and for students to communicate with a wide range of audiences.

A flexible communications tool for archiving asynchronous communication is the online discussion board. Schools are using web-based learning management systems such as *Blackboard* or the free *Moodle* to share web resources, assignment and lesson summaries, online quizzes, grade books, and other tools among teachers and students. Parents can even log in and see a student's grades at any time during the term. These learning management systems also include a discussion board where teachers, students, parents, community experts, distant students, or government leaders can discuss topics and work on projects collaboratively, but in relative privacy. Users must be added to the discussion and must log in to participate.

Clips from the Classroom DVD Activity 5.1: The Internet for Learning
Discussion boards are used for homework help, for debates on controversial topics, and for group sharing of information. In the "Internet and Virtual Schools" section of the *Clips for the Classroom* DVD, you'll see three settings where students use websites created for them by their teachers. As you watch the video clips listed in the table, consider and do the following:
- Make note of ways the class websites connect the students to the world beyond their class.
- List ideas of how the classes might make use of a discussion board for learning.

☉ Clip	How does the class website connect students to the world beyond the class?	How can the class use a discussion board for learning?
Online and Face-to-Face High School		
Learning Online		
Virtual English Course		
Virtual Geometry Course		
EZ Geometry Website Supports Student Work		

Project-based learning

To further transform learning and engage students in acquiring 21st century skills, teachers use project-based learning. Students become immersed in projects designed around real-world challenges in which they explore open-ended situations, involving work that is often collaborative. In addition, project-based learning values multiple sources of information and performance assessment (Esch, 1998), ideally supported by technology.

A goal of project-based learning is creation of a product or artifact. Project-based learning leads students through project development stages that are meant to reflect real-world practices. The knowledge, skills, and dispositions acquired in the process are equal in value to the end result itself. Project-based learning provides a context in which students move toward thinking as an expert in the knowledge domain might think because the students learn in the process of creating an authentic, realistic project modeled on a project an expert or professional might create. Students draw from many examples of performance, evaluate and synthesize information from many sources, and incorporate alternative viewpoints.

Approximately ten years of studies have been conducted studying project-based learning at the K-12 level, with positive results (Thomas, 2000). Examples of technology-supported project-based learning are the many WebQuests that teachers have developed for their students, and project-based competitions such as ThinkQuest that encourage team efforts and collaboration among students.

In contrast to project-based learning, problem-based learning uses an inquiry approach to solve a complex, realistic problem. Students present their conclusions, which may or may not include a solution. Problem-based learning is at its core a process-oriented experience, and technology is well suited to improve access to the information and tools needed to work through the problem-solving process.

National Educational Technology Standards for Students (NETS-S) Question

Give three examples of NETS-S standards that are well suited to project-based learning experiences that integrate technology, and include your reasons for choosing each standard.

Clips from the Classroom DVD Activity 5.2: Problem-Based Learning

In the two clips listed from the "Software and Media" theme of the ***Clips from the Classroom*** DVD, students must solve a realistic problem that requires thinking skills and technology tools.

Video clips for this question:
- Challenger Center Provides Problem-based Learning
- Challenger Center Youth Leadership

As you watch the video clips listed above, consider and do the following.

- Note the problem the students encounter, and the ways technology is used in the problem-solving process.
- Note the types of learning the students and the student leaders experience as they take on the role of problem solver.
- What are the students learning?
- What are the student leaders learning?
- What is another example of a realistic problem that students could solve using technology in a classroom?

SAMPLE RESPONSES TO VIDEO DISCUSSION and NETS-S QUESTIONS IN CHAPTER 1

THEME 1: Transforming Teaching and Learning

1. Technology is used in teaching and learning for many purposes, such as increasing student interest and motivation for learning, increasing student time spent interacting with content, addressing a fuller range of student learning styles, providing professional tools for student work, and helping students to develop skills in evaluation and communication. What are some of the benefits the students get from technology in the classrooms shown in the clips?

> Valarie Young's students encounter the history that they learn by using multiple information sources, media types, and sensory channels. The benefits to students are that the students interact with the course content repeatedly and they access information in ways that address varied learning styles. They also have social experiences working with concepts as whole groups, small groups, and individuals. The students in the tablet classrooms have the same benefits. In addition, they have opportunities to engage in "cognitive apprenticeship" when they observe the teacher and other students demonstrating their thought processes by working on problems in front of the class.

2. Valarie Young and Mary Lynn Smith chose technology to address learning problems that they identified in their classes. Describe a learning problem from one of the classes, and explain how technology was used in the solution to the problem.

> Valarie teaches a very visual subject. Learning history involves understanding geographic settings, studying the art and artifacts of cultures, and knowing the techniques of historians and archaeologists. Valarie takes advantage of her students' interest in visual media to show them images, maps, and film using technology. She builds the stories of history on the visual elements to give her students a three-dimensional perception of the subject. Mary Lynn needs her students to practice hearing, speaking, and reading the language they are learning. She keeps students' interest in practicing by asking verbal questions, and by using the text projected from the tablet that students can analyze together.

3. Technology is best used in a classroom when it has a relative advantage over a non-technology approach. Select a technology in use in one of the classrooms shown in the clips, and discuss the advantage that the technology has over teaching without the technology.

> In both Valarie's and Mary Lynn's classes, the computer and projector replace several other pieces of equipment, including an overhead projector, videotape player, chalkboard, and maps. The advantage is that the information that was previously separated by media type is now connected in the computer, enabling the class to move quickly and easily among media as appropriate, without being limited by the availability of several devices. For students, this connection among media strengthens the natural conceptual connections they make in learning.

National Educational Technology Standards for Students (NETS-S) Question

In each clip students have more interaction with the technology and they have more visual examples of information.

THEME 2: Software and Media

1. In these classrooms, technology has been placed in the hands of first through twelfth grade students. Thinking about two of the classrooms, describe how student access to technology has changed the way the classroom operates. What is the same? What is different?

   In the fifth grade classrooms of Cunningham Creek Elementary School, the students always have their networked laptop computers. The teachers have changed the assignments they give so the work is done using software and Internet tools rather than paper, pencil, and reference materials. The assignments also require synthesis of more varied types of information. Students have immediate access to a wider range of tools in their laptops, enabling them to work more independently and at higher levels of thinking than they could without the laptops. Prior to the establishment of the Challenger Center, students did not have the immersive simulation in which to learn about working in space. The teachers in the students' regular classroom and in the Center have changed to teaching in greater depth about the knowledge and skills the student will develop in the simulation. Mike Patterson has developed geometry challenges that his students solve using technology including software and a website. These changes give the students materials they can use inside and outside of class, and they allow students to try approaches to problems more quickly and independently than they could by using more traditional methods. In the first and fourth grade classes at the Bolles School, the teachers have helped their students to learn math skills and social studies content by developing electronic presentations. The teaching and learning processes have changed because the materials used by students have changed, and the ways of demonstrating learning and communicating have changed.

2. Each clip shows students using a specific software tool for learning. Describe how three of the software tools supports learning.

   Amy Eisler's students use a word processing program to organize and report on their observations. The software helps the students to create tables and text more quickly than they can on paper, and it allows more efficient editing and sharing of information among students. In addition, when students use the Internet to research the topic, they can easily integrate the Internet information into their work. The *Quizdom* software gives Shelly Couch instant information about the concepts students know well and those that students find difficult. This immediate information helps her to use the class time to focus on areas where students need the most help. The Challenger Center's simulation software allows students to take on real-world responsibilities and to learn in a realistic context that engages every student. The software gives the students experience in applying their classroom knowledge to a novel problem-solving situation. Mike Patterson's students use geometric construction software to learn about the properties of plane figures in a way that encourages exploration and creativity and also makes students independent learners. The presentation software in the elementary grade classrooms is used by students to collect, organize, and communicate information to an audience, all of which are valuable skills.

3. In addition to learning content area standards, what other learning is experienced by students in one of the technology-rich classrooms shown on the DVD? Can you identify specific content standards addressed in the classroom by referring to state or national standards for a content area?

   In technology-rich classrooms, students learn technology skills. They may learn communication skills if they use the technology to communicate by writing or speaking to others. Because most of the work done with computers is text-based, students develop reading skills when they work with technology. Students can learn about other cultures. They can develop creativity, group skills, and other 21st century skills.

In Amy Eisler's lesson, elementary life science standards related to heredity are addressed. Shelly Couch's lesson addresses elementary math standards related to display of data. The students at the Challenger Center are meeting middle school standards in math and science, in particular those related to using data to solve problems and the study of processes that shape the earth. The geometry students are learning the high school math standards for properties of plane figures. Caryn Canfield's fourth grade students are learning the elementary social studies standards for state history and ecosystems, and **language** arts standards for spoken and written communication as well as research skills. Jennifer Salley's first grade students are learning elementary math number sense and arithmetic, and communication.

4. Teachers establish rituals and routines with their students to help the learning process flow smoothly. For example, a middle school teacher may limit student movement to pencil sharpeners and rest rooms to specific times, and an elementary teacher may request that students use ink and cursive handwriting for final drafts of work. What routines do you observe in these classrooms that relate to the use of technology by students?

Amy Eisler instructs her students when to use the computers and when to attend to other activities. She asks students to close the laptop lids when they are ready for the next activity. In Shelly Couch's class, students work individually on their laptops, quietly helping each other when help is needed. When her students use the quiz system, they respond to the question quietly, and then discuss the question after a student has been called on to give the answer. At the Challenger Center, each student has a specific role and responsibility with instructions to follow. Students ask the older student assistants for help. Mike Patterson's students work with partners on problems, and individually on their computer projects, asking him for help when they reach a confusing point. He helps them to solve the problem, rather than giving them answers. In the elementary tablet classrooms, students take turns using the tablet, giving their attention to the student who controls the computer.

National Educational Technology Standards for Students (NETS-S) Questions

1. In "Laptops for Data in Fifth Grade," the students practice skills in information literacy and communication. In "Challenger Center Youth Leadership," students learn to collaborate with other peers and to solve problems as they acquire experience in an area of personal interest.

2. Students at the Challenger Learning Center work on problems requiring use of information and collaboration with others. The problems relate to mechanical and earth systems.

THEME 3: The Internet and Virtual Schools

1. The Internet is used for several purposes by the teachers in these clips. Discuss one purpose for using the Internet for learning in each classroom featured in the clips. Then, discuss the reasons the teachers or students have for choosing to use the Internet as a tool for learning.

At the Odyssey Charter High School, the Internet was selected as the primary delivery medium for the school because it gave students a flexible and individualized alternative to neighborhood school and home school. The Internet is used for all aspects of education, including completing and submitting assignments, taking tests, managing grades, and giving instructions. Students also communicate with teachers and each other, and access information and multimedia resources using the Internet. Florida Virtual School students use the Internet for the same purposes. The students choose the Internet for their education because they need to take a course not offered in their regular school, they prefer learning via technology, they need a non-traditional calendar or schedule, or they are unable to attend another school. The purpose of using the Internet in Valarie Young's class is to have access to media, including movies for enhancing the learning of history. Valarie's students also use professional primary source documents on websites because they are easily and widely accessible via the web inside and outside of class. Mike Patterson's geometry students solve problems of the month and access class notes on the course website. The web is used to give students information and help outside of class so they do not need to wait until class time.

2. Students learning in public virtual schools are expected to meet the same academic standards as students in traditional public schools, but the methods used for teaching and learning are different. How is the virtual school experience shown in the two virtual schools on the DVD different from your classroom experience for students and for teachers?

For some virtual school students, they only know classmates online. The students know their teachers on an individual basis and can ask questions almost any time of day by e-mail or telephone. Students can work according to their own timeline, and they need to use self-discipline and motivation to keep up with expectations. Students may be distant from their classmates, and they have more time for involvement in activities outside of school. Time spent on schoolwork is spent reading, writing, and working on assignments, in contrast to time in classrooms that involves more listening and speaking.

National Educational Technology Standards for Students (NETS-S) Questions

1. The students have developed positive attitudes toward educational technology as a result of their increased independence and flexibility as learners, the individual respect and attention they have from teachers, and the opportunities they have to pursue their own interests instead of conforming to the structure of a campus-based school.

2. The productivity tools used in the classes include word processors and publishing tools. The communications tools include the telephone, e-mail, online discussion, chat, and file sharing tools. The research tools include the Internet. The problem-solving and decision-making tools include geometric visualization and manipulation tools.

3. In "Scholarly Writings Online Engage Students," students evaluate web-based information and report results using technology as they investigate a problem of credibility in the humanities. In "EZ Geometry Website Supports Student Work," students locate information and process data using technology as they work on mathematical problems. In both clips, students use technology to prepare to solve problems, although the nature of the problems varies.

THEME 4: Technology across the Curriculum

1. Choose three of the classrooms from this theme and discuss the following:
   - An educational problem that was addressed with technology,
   - The technology that was used, and
   - The relative advantage offered by the technology over using a non-technology approach to the problem.

a. Patty Kmieciak addresses the problem of developing student understanding and analysis of literature by using presentation software. The technology added to the students' engagement in the lesson, provided a structure for student participation, and guided students with increasingly difficult questions about their reading.

b. Kate Pritchard used the language lab to address the need for students to have extensive time reading, writing, speaking, and listening as they learn German. The advantage offered by the technology is that it helps students to focus their attention on their learning and the headphones reduce distractions. In addition, students spend the majority of their time in direct communication.

c. The trigonometry students in Mike Patterson's class use technology to address the problem of understanding the concepts behind graphing equations. The graphing calculator is a tool that each student uses to test his or her ideas about the causes of the changes in the graphs for different equations. The calculator overhead display has the advantage of allowing students to share the work they have done individually by using the same tool for group discussion.

d. Students in Don Page's world history class are focused on the problem of understanding the factors influencing events and cultures in Greek history. The advantages offered by the tablet computer and projector are that Don can display a variety of visual images from any electronic source to make the subject more vivid and memorable, he can annotate and illustrate the maps and pictures as the class discusses the events, and the whole class can easily see the material.

e. Richard Chamberlain's photography students are working on the problem of learning and applying the techniques of a prominent photographer by using the Internet and digital image editing software. The images from the photographer's website can be viewed and analyzed by the class, and students can view them later individually. The image editing software is used by the students to immediately develop their skills with the techniques. The students are using professional tools.

f. The problems addressed in Lynn Howard's music theory class are to identify and compose using specific musical styles and components. The MIDI hardware and composition software offer the students a system for creating, seeing, and hearing the music, and they offer the teacher a way of checking student learning during class and evaluating student products.

g. The *SmartBoards* used at the Florida School for the Deaf and Blind address the problems of language learning by students with disabilities. Because the students in the classes of Colette Cook and Teresa Smith are deaf or hard of hearing, they rely heavily on visual tools for learning. The advantages of the *SmartBoard* include its large size, its ability to respond to text or images, and its interactive nature, all of which engage students and offer many opportunities for practice.

2. Imagine that you are a teacher in two of the classrooms in this theme. Think about the following:

- What would you say to the parents of your students to help them understand how you use technology in your class?
- What would you say to visiting members of the school board?

The technology used in the class gives the students a richer, more realistic, multi-sensory, and engaging experience that results in deeper learning because the students are more engaged and their learning styles are addressed. In addition to learning the subject matter, the students learn important 21st century skills in ways that they understand.

National Educational Technology Standards for Students (NETS-S) Questions

1. In the Episcopal High School language lab, students enhance their learning by analyzing their own and others' speech, by engaging in extended oral practice, and by receiving feedback from the teacher. They use telecommunications tools to communicate with peers and the teacher.

2. The trigonometry students are developing their abilities to solve mathematical problems, to use a variety of tools, to cooperate with others in solving problems, and to communicate the results of problem solving.

SAMPLE RESPONSES TO VIDEO DISCUSSION QUESTIONS and NETS-S QUESTIONS IN CHAPTER 2

National Educational Technology Standards for Students (NETS-S) Question (p. 21)

Information Age Ability	NETS-S Standards
work is knowledge-oriented	3, 4, 5
workers are learners needing flexible, advanced skill sets for rapid innovation	2, 5, 6
workgroups identify and solve problems over extended time periods, then communicate results	4, 5, 6

The 21st Century Skills (p. 26)

1. Digital-Age Literacy
   - Basic, scientific, economic, and technological literacies: NETS-S 2-6
   - Visual and information literacies: NETS-S 3-4
   - Multicultural literacy and global awareness: NETS-S 2-6
2. Inventive Thinking
   - Adaptability and managing complexity: NETS-S 5-6
   - Self-direction: NETS-S 1-2
   - Curiosity, creativity, and risk taking: NETS-S 3, 4, 6
   - Higher-order thinking and sound reasoning: NETS-S 2, 5, 6
3. Effective Communication
   - Teaming, collaboration, and interpersonal skills: NETS-S 2, 4
   - Personal, social, and civic responsibility: NETS-S 2, 4
   - Interactive communication: NETS-S 4
4. High Productivity
   - Prioritizing, planning, and managing for results: NETS-S 4-6
   - Effective use of real-world tools: NETS-S 3-6
   - Ability to produce relevant, high-quality products: NETS-S 3-6

DVD Activity 2.1. In the clip "Secondary Students Respond Positively," Valarie Young integrates multimedia and many opportunities for student interaction into her lessons. In "Laptops and Data in Fifth Grade," the teachers use a variety of hands-on activities that allow the students to have control, make choices, and manipulate information. In "E-Z Geometry Website Supports Student Work," Mike Patterson gives students anywhere, anytime access to assistance and practice with the course material, as well as tools for communication among several audiences.

DVD Activity 2.2.

Clip	Skills	Role of Technology
Laptops for Data in Fifth Grade	Keyboarding, reading and writing, communicating data, data analysis, teamwork, speaking and listening, knowledge of subject matter, use of software tools, information and media literacy	Tools for writing and displaying data
Challenger Center Provides Problem-Based Learning	Reading and writing, communicating data, data analysis, problem solving, teamwork, speaking and listening, knowledge of subject matter, use of software tools	Communication media, tools for working with data, information reference
Challenger Center Youth Leadership	Reading and writing, communicating data, data analysis, problem solving, teamwork, speaking and listening, knowledge of subject matter, use of software tools, leadership	Communication media, tools for working with data, information reference
Tablet Computers in Fourth Grade Science	Keyboarding, reading and writing, speaking and listening, knowledge of subject matter, use of software tools, information and media literacy	Information reference, tools for writing and organizing media
Tablet Computers in First Grade Mathematics	Keyboarding, reading and writing, speaking and listening, knowledge of subject matter, use of software tools, information and media literacy	Tools for writing and organizing media
Online and Face-to-Face High School	Reading and writing, knowledge of subject matter, use of software tools, information and media literacy	Information reference, tools for writing and organizing media, communication media
Learning Online	Reading and writing, knowledge of subject matter, use of software tools, information and media literacy	Information reference, tools for writing and organizing media, communication media
Virtual English Course	Keyboarding, reading and writing, knowledge of subject matter, use of software tools, information and media literacy	Information reference, tools for writing and organizing media, communication media
Virtual Geometry Course	Keyboarding, reading and writing, knowledge of subject matter, use of software tools, information and media literacy	Information reference, tools for writing and organizing media, tools for working with data, communication media
Virtual School Philosophy	Reading and writing, knowledge of subject matter, use of software tools, information and media literacy	Information reference, tools for writing and organizing media, tools for working with data, communication media

SAMPLE RESPONSES TO VIDEO DISCUSSION QUESTIONS IN CHAPTER 3

DVD Activity 3.1. Mike Patterson's students are developing the following higher-order skills though the use of *Geometer's Sketchpad*: analysis, comparison, inference, evaluation.

DVD Activity 3.2 In "Student Achievement Increases," both the whole group and small group uses of technology work well for giving students a common foundation of knowledge and for giving them opportunities to apply the knowledge in projects and assignments. The multimedia elements of the class present information using multiple modalities and senses.

In "Tablet Computers Facilitate Learning," both the teacher-directed and hands-on uses of technology work to engage and motivate students, as well as to aid in learning through the use of multimedia and interaction.

In "Website and *Photoshop* in Photography," both the whole group and small group uses of technology work well for giving students a common foundation of knowledge and for giving them opportunities to apply the knowledge in projects and assignments.

DVD Activity 3.3.

Examples	Technology or non-technology	Reasons for choosing
Greek Geography question	Non-technology	Individual/pair accountability, can be done quickly, can be adapted for time and student needs
CD-ROM textbook activity	Technology	Uses multimedia and allows student choice of information, uses authentic sources of information, students can work at their own pace

DVD Activity 3.4. In "*Quizdom* System for Practice," the students are involved in interpersonal communication because the technology is used in a group activity. The technology is integrated with curriculum and assessment, and it provides feedback.

In "Composition Software and MIDI in Music," students are using technology in a creative activity that is integrated with curriculum. The technology is part of the regular activities of the class.

In "*SmartBoards* for Hearing Impaired Students," there is physical activity involved in using the technology, and it is used with interpersonal communication. The technology is integrated with curriculum and assessment, and is part of regular class activities. It is also used with text and images.

DVD Activity 3.5. In general, the teachers in the clips have the goals of using technology to increase student learning by making the learning more engaging and by giving students a wider range of tools for learning using a variety of strategies. In each clip the specific tools and strategies vary. Each teacher has reduced the paper-based work happening in the class and increased the digital work.

SAMPLE RESPONSES TO VIDEO DISCUSSION QUESTIONS IN CHAPTER 4

DVD Activity 4.1. Patty's <u>needs assessment</u> may have helped her realize that her students were having difficulty understanding and remembering the events and themes of the literature they read, and she identified a technological solution to this problem. She <u>planned instruction</u> that would include the multimedia presentation that she designed to engage her students and help them learn the concepts. She did the <u>logistical</u> work of ensuring that the classroom had a screen, projector, computer with the presentation file, and power outlets for the equipment. She located places for the equipment and places for the student seating so students could see and hear. She <u>prepared</u> the computer by saving the presentation on it and connecting it to the projector, and then she ensured that all of the elements of the lessons worked together. She explained the lesson to the students and identified the students who would be players. She <u>taught</u> the lesson, and may have done reflective revisions for the next time she uses it.

DVD Activity 4.2. Valaric learned to use technology in her classes by learning from family members and colleagues in informal sessions. She also attended formal professional development classes to acquire skills. The strategies that worked for her were to learn skills from others and then to practice the skills in the context of her teaching.

DVD Activity 4.3. Mike uses directed learning when he is demonstrating a problem on the board for the class and guiding the class through a common practice problem. He uses constructivist activities when he gives the students general instructions and asks them to find a solution on their own using the tools and assistance in the classroom. He assesses student learning through problem-solving practice and through hands-on projects. The NETS-S standards addressed during the directed learning activities include the development of positive attitudes toward technology and employment of technology in development of strategies for solving problems, and those that apply to the constructivist activities include elements of standards 1-6.

DVD Activity 4.4. Valarie uses practice questions for pairs of students, short quizzes, questions that students answer while using the Internet, group projects, and informal class discussions to assess student understanding. The practice questions, quizzes, and discussions are formative, and the group projects and Internet projects are summative. The questions answered in pairs and class discussions give students the real-world skills of interpersonal communication, and the higher-order skills of analysis, comparison, inference and interpretation, evaluation, and synthesis. The Internet and group projects give students the real-world skills of organization and planning, use of multiple communication media, information literacy, and teamwork. Those assignments also give students the higher-order skills of analysis, comparison, inference and interpretation, evaluation, and synthesis.

DVD Activity 4.5. In each class, the computer is used in whole group activities when new information is presented and discussed as a group. The benefits are that students encounter many viewpoints on the material, and large amounts of information can be presented in short periods of time. The class uses computers for small group activities to practice and apply knowledge. The advantage is that each student can be accountable for his or her work, and students can make choices of topics and materials.

DVD Activity 4.6. In "Technology Manages Flow of Activities," Valarie thinks ahead about how to combine and order the different technologies and techniques to make the subject matter engaging and logical. She prepares her presentations with images, links to websites that reinforce the concepts, video, and practice questions. She times the activities to ensure that there will be time for all activities. Few of the NETS-S standards are addressed when Valarie is leading discussions with the whole group, while most of the standards can be met when the students work hands-on with the computers.

In "Laptops for Data in Fifth Grade," Amy and Shelly understand that common skills are needed for different computer applications. They instruct students when to open and close their laptop lids when activities change. They have worked with their students on following routines for whole group and small group activities, so students know when they should be using the computer. The majority of the NETS-S are addressed through the combination of teacher-centered and student-centered activities in these classes.

In "Graphing Calculators in Trigonometry," Mike Patterson instructs students when to work independently and when to share information with partners. He uses the whiteboards so students can document and share the work they do on the calculators. He also connects calculators to an overhead display. The majority of the NETS-S are addressed through the combination of teacher-centered and student-centered activities in this class.

SAMPLE RESPONSES TO VIDEO DISCUSSION QUESTIONS and NETS-S QUESTION IN CHAPTER 5

DVD Activity 5.1. In each class, the websites connect students to course content and web-based information, and it enables communication with teachers and other students. The web also connects students with experts in the subject. Students could use a discussion board to share questions, problems, and solutions related to course assignments. A discussion board could also be used to invite "guest speakers" to a class discussion.

DVD Activity 5.2. At the Challenger Learning Center, students work on problems related to weather and to the functioning of the space station. They use technology to collect data about the problems, to communicate data with other students, and to work on solutions to the problems. Students learn teamwork and communication skills as they depend on each other and others depend on them to solve the problems in the scenario. The students are learning real-world skills of communicating and working with others and higher-order skills as they interpret information. They are learning about the interdisciplinary nature of science and the work of NASA. The student leaders are learning how to communicate with others effectively.

National Educational Technology Standards for Students (NETS-S) Question (p. 54)
In project-based learning experiences that integrate technology, students can achieve all NETS-S standards. Project-based learning is particularly well suited to address standards 5 and 6 because of the focus on student-directed research on a real-world problem.

RESOURCES

REFERENCES

Alexander, P. (2003). The development of expertise. *Education Researcher,* 32(9), 10–14.

Apple Computer. (1995). ACOT's 10-year report. Accessed November 27, 2004, from
    http://images.apple.com/education/k12/leadership/acot/pdf/10yr.pdf

Bayraktar, S. (2001-2002). A meta-analysis of the effectiveness of computer-assisted instruction in
    science education. *Journal of Research on Technology in Education,* 34, 173–188.

Becker, J. (2001). How are teachers using computers in instruction? Paper presented at the annual
    meeting of the American Association of Educational Research. Accessed December 6, 2004,
    from http://www.crito.uci.edu/tlc/FINDINGS/special3/How_Are_Teachers_Using.pdf

Becker, H. (2000). Who's wired and who's not: Children's access to and use of computer
    technology. *The Future of Children,* 10(2),56.

Bransford, J., Brown, A., & Cocking, R. (Eds.). (1999). *How people learn.* Washington, DC: National
    Academy Press.

Calhoun, E. (1994). *How to use action research in the self-renewing school.* Alexandria, VA: Association for
    Supervision and Curriculum Development.

Cavanaugh, C. S. (2001). The effectiveness of interactive distance education technologies in K-12
    learning: A meta-analysis. *International Journal of Educational Telecommunications,* 7, 73–88.

CEO Forum on Education and Technology. (2001). The CEO Forum school technology and
    readiness report: Key building blocks for student achievement in the 21st century. Retrieved
    November 26, 2004, from http://www.ceoforum.org/downloads/report4.pdf

Christmann, E., & Badgett, J. (1999). A comparative analysis of the effects of computer-assisted
    instruction on student achievement in differing science and demographical areas. *Journals of
    Computers in Mathematics and Science Teaching,* 18, 135–143.

Conte, C. (1997). Learning connection: Schools in the Information Age. Accessed October 23, 2004,
    from http://www.benton.org/publibrary/schools/connection.html

DeBell, M., & Chapman, C. (2002). Computer and Internet use by children and adolescents in 2001.
    National Center for Education Statistics. Accessed December 6, 2004, from
    http://nces.ed.gov/programs/quarterly/vol_5/5_4/2_1.asp

Education Week. (2001a). Dividing Lines. *Education Week,* Vol. 20(35), pp. 12-13. Accessed December 6,
    2004, from http://counts.edweek.org/sreports/tc01/tc01article.cfm?slug=35divideintro.h20

Education Week. (2001b). Technology Counts 2001: The new digital divides. *Education Week,* May 10, 2001.

Esch, C. (1998). Project-based or problem-based: The same or different? Accessed December 9, 2004, from http://pblmm.k12.ca.us/PBLGuide/PBL&PBL.htm

Gehring, J. (2001). Not enough girls. *Education Week,* 20, (35), 18–19. Accessed December 6, 2004, from http://counts.edweek.org/sreports/tc01/tc01article.cfm?slug=35girls.h20

Geisert, P., & Futrell, M. (1995). *Teachers, computers and curriculum: Microcomputers in the classroom.* Needham Heights, MA: Allyn & Bacon.

Goodlad, J., Mantle-Bromley, C., & Goodlad, S. (2004). *Education for everyone.* San Francisco: Jossey-Bass.

Holcomb, E. (1999). *Getting excited about data: How to combine people, passion and proof.* Thousand Oaks, CA: Corwin Press, Inc.

Hord, S. M., Rutherford, W. L., Huling-Austin, L. and Hall, G. E. (1987). *Taking charge of change.* Austin, TX: Southwest Educational Development Laboratory.

International Society for Technology in Education. (2000). *National Educational Technology Standards for Teachers.* Accessed November 21, 2004, from http://cnets.iste.org/teachers/t_stands.html

Jaffe, D. (2003). Virtual transformation: Web-based technology and pedagogical change. *Teaching Sociology* 31, (2), 227–236.

Jonassen, D., Howland, J., Moore, J., Marra, R. (2003). *Learning to solve problems with technology: A constructivist perspective.* (2nd ed.). Upper Saddle River, NJ: Merrill/Prentice Hall.

Kulik, J. (2003). Effects of using instructional technology in elementary and secondary schools: What controlled evaluation studies say. SRI International. Retrieved November 26, 2004, from http://www.sri.com/policy/csted/reports/sandt/it/Kulik_ITinK-12_Main_Report.pdf

Lanahan, L. (2002). Beyond school-level Internet access: Support for instructional use of technology. National Center for Education Statistics 2002029. Accessed December 6, 2004, from http://nces.ed.gov/surveys/frss/publications/2002029/

Lee, J. (1999). Effectiveness of computer-based instructional simulation: A meta-analysis. *International Journal of Instructional Media,* 26, 71-85.

Lou, Y., Abrami, P. C., & d'Apollonia, S. (2001). Small group and individual learning with technology: A meta-analysis. *Review of Educational Research,* 71, 449-521.

Mayer, R. (2001). *Multimedia learning.* New York: Cambridge University Press.

McLean, J. (1995). *Improving education through action research: A guide for administrators and teachers.* Thousand Oaks, CA: Corwin Press.

McNiff, J., Lomax, P., & Whitehead, J. (2003). *You and your action research project.* London: Hyde Publications.

Morrison, G., & Lowther, D. (2005). *Integrating computer technology into the classroom* (3rd ed.). Upper Saddle River, NJ: Merrill/Prentice Hall.

Mills, G. (2003). *Action research: A guide for the teacher researcher* (2nd ed.). Upper Saddle River, NJ: Merrill/Prentice Hall.

Murphy, R., Penuel, W., Means, B., Korbak, C., Whaley, A., & Allen, J. (2002). E-DESK: A review of recent evidence on discrete educational software. SRI International. Accessed November 26, 2004, from http://ctl.sri.com/publications/downloads/Task3_FinalReport3.pdf

Murray, C. (2004, July). In educational technology, leaders matter most. *eSchool News*, pp. 1–2.

National Center for Educational Statistics. (2002). Beyond school-level internet access: Support for instructional use of technology. Washington, DC: U.S. Department of Education. Online at http://nces.ed.gov/surveys/frss/publications/2002029/

Nisan-Nelson, P. (2001). Technology integration: A case of professional development. *Journal of Technology and Teacher Education, 9*, 83-103. Accessed November 27, 2004, from Available: http://dl.aace.org/6394

Osterman, K., & Kottkamp, R. (1993). *Reflective practice for educators: Improving schooling through professional development.* Newbury Park, CA: Corwin Press.

Papert, S. (1996). *The connected family: Bridging the digital generation gap.* Athens, GA: Longstreet Press.

Roblyer, M. (2006). *Integrating educational technology into teaching* (4th ed.). Upper Saddle River, NJ: Merrill/Prentice Hall.

Rose, D., & Dalton, B. (2002). Using technology to individualize reading instruction. In C.C. Block, L. B. Gambrell & M. Pressley (Eds.), *Improving comprehension instruction: Rethinking research, theory, and classroom practice* (pp. 257–274). San Francisco: Jossey Bass.

Technology Counts 2001: The new divides: Looking beneath the numbers to reveal digital inequities. (2001). *Education Week* 20(35).

Thomas, J. (2000). A review of research on project-based learning. The Autodesk Foundation. Accessed December 9, 2004, from http://www.autodesk.com/foundation

U.S. Department of Education. (2001). *Teachers' tools for the 21st century: A report on teachers' use of technology.* Washington, DC: National Center for Education Statistics.

U.S. Department of Education. (2004). Structure: General information. Accessed December 6, 2004, from http://www.ed.gov/about/offices/list/ous/international/usnei/us/edlite-struc-geninfo.html

Valdez, G., McNabb, M., Foertsch, M., Anderson, M., Hawkes, M., & Raack, L. (2000). Computer-based technology and learning: Evolving uses and expectations. North Central Regional Educational Laboratory. Accessed November 28, 2004, from http://www.ncrel.org/tplan/cbtl/toc.htm

Waxman, H., Lin, M., & Michko, G. (2003). A meta-analysis of the effectiveness of teaching and learning with technology on student outcomes. Accessed November 26, 2004, from http://www.ncrel.org/tech/effects2/index.html

Wenglinsky, H. (1998). Does it compute? The relationship between educational technology and student achievement in mathematics. Educational Testing Service. Retrieved November 26, 2004, from ftp://ftp.ets.org/pub/res/technolog.pdf

WEBLIOGRAPHY

Millennial Students, Technology Standards, and 21ˢᵗ Century Skills
- Millennials Rising. http://www.millennialsrising.com/
- National Educational Technology Plan. http://www.nationaledtechplan.org/default.asp
- Partnership for 21ˢᵗ Century Skills. http://www.21stcenturyskills.org
- Pew Internet and American Life Project. http://www.pewinternet.org
- Students in Today's Schools. http://www.nationaledtechplan.org/docs_and_pdf/john_netp_12503.pdf
- World Peace through Technology. http://www.peacetour.org

Action Research
- Action Research International online journal. http://www.scu.edu.au/schools/gcm/ar/ari/arihome.html
- Collaborative Action Research Network. http://www.did.stu.mmu.ac.uk/carn/
- Definitions and bibliography from NCREL. http://www.ncrel.org/sdrs/areas/issues/envrnmnt/drugfree/sa3act.htm
- Guide for the Teacher Researcher from Geoff Mills. http://www.sou.edu/EDUCATION/action_research.htm
- Overview from Access Excellence. http://www.ncrel.org/sdrs/areas/issues/envrnmnt/drugfree/sa3act.htm

Technology Effectiveness
- 5 Myths About Kids Writing with Computers. http://familyeducation.com/article/0,1120,1-260,00.html
- Computers Make Kids Smarter, Right? http://www.technos.net/journal/volume7/2cuban.htm
- The Costs and Effectiveness of Educational Technology. http://www.ed.gov/Technology/Plan/RAND/Costs/costs4.html

- Evaluating the Effectiveness of Educational Technology.
  http://millennium.aed.org/fulton.shtml
- The Impact of Technology. http://www.mcrel.org/products/tech/technology/impact.asp
- Plugging In: Choosing and Using Educational Technology.
  http://www.ncrel.org/sdrs/edtalk/toc.htm
- Research in Educational Technology. http://www.edtechnot.com/notresearch.html
- Teacher and Teacher-Directed Student Use of Computers and Software.
  http://www.crito.uci.edu/tlc/findings/computeruse/
- Teacher Universe Research Studies. http://www.teacheruniverse.com/news/research.html
- Tech LEARNING.
  http://www.techlearning.com/db_area/archives/TL/062000/archives/interv.html
- Technology and Education Reform Report Executive Summary from the U.S. Department
  of Education. http://www.ed.gov/pubs/SER/Technology
- Technology Counts. http://www.edweek.org/ew/index.html
- Technology Effectiveness Framework. http://www.ncrel.org/sdrs/edtalk/tef.htm
- Technology: How Do We Know It Works?
  http://www.ed.gov/Technology/TechConf/1999/whitepapers/paper5.html
- Technology in America's Schools: Seven Dimensions for Gauging Progress from Milken
  Family Foundation. http://www.mff.org/edtech
- Using Technology to Improve Student Achievement.
  http://www.ncrel.org/sdrs/areas/issues/methods/technlgy/te800.htm

Effective Professional Development
- Creating Time for Staff Development.
  http://www.ncrel.org/sdrs/areas/issues/educatrs/profdevl/pd3lk6.htm
- Critical Issue: Finding the Time for Professional Development.
  http://www.ncrel.org/sdrs/areas/issues/educatrs/profdevl/pd300.htm
- Educational Technology: Support for Inquiry-Based Learning.
  http://ra.terc.edu/publications/TERC_pubs/tech-infusion/ed_tech/ed_tech_frame.html
- Eisenhower National Clearinghouse Professional Development.
  http://www.enc.org/weblinks/pd/
- Jamie MacKenzie's Staff Development. http://staffdevelop.org
- Making Technology Happen: Best Practices and Policies from K-12 Schools.
  http://www.southern.org/edtech/chapter4.htm
- National Staff Development Council. http://www.nsdc.org/
- National Center for Technology Planning. http://www.nctp.com/
- NCREL Professional Development. http://www.ncrel.org/pd/
- Professional Development in a Technological Age: New Definitions, Old Challenges, New
  Resources. http://ra.terc.edu/publications/TERC_pubs/tech-
  infusion/prof_dev/prof_dev_frame.html
- Results Oriented Professional Development.
  http://www.ncrel.org/sdrs/areas/rpl_esys/pdlitrev.htm#Introduction

Rubrics
- About.com Rubric page. http://7-12educators.about.com/education/7-
  12educators/cs/rubrics/index.htm
- Assessment Toolkit. http://www.nwrel.org/eval/toolkit98/
- Discovery School Rubric page. http://discoveryschool.com/schrockguide/assess.html

- 🌐 Midlink Magazine's Rubrics. http://www.ncsu.edu/midlink/ho.html
- 🌐 Rubric Bank. http://intranet.cps.k12.il.us/Assessments/Ideas_and_Rubrics/Rubric_Bank/rubric_bank.html
- 🌐 Rubric Construction Set. http://www.landmark-project.com/classweb/rubrics/
- 🌐 Rubric Generators. http://www.teach-nology.com/web_tools/rubrics/
- 🌐 Rubric Template. http://edweb.sdsu.edu/triton/july/rubrics/Rubric_Template.html

Organizing and Managing Technology
- 🌐 Building Block model for Integrated Technology Projects. http://www.essdack.org/tool/bbmodel.html
- 🌐 Building-Level Technology Plans. http://www.nctp.com/html/plan_building.cfm
- 🌐 Commandments of Technology Implementation. http://www.techlearning.com/db_area/archives/WCE/archives/collette.htm
- 🌐 Coordinators Influencing Teachers. http://www.techlearning.com/db_area/archives/WCE/archives/afisher.htm
- 🌐 Hosting a School Technology Fair. http://www.techlearning.com/db_area/archives/WCE/archives/nelsontf.htm
- 🌐 Integrated Technology Projects Database and Template Form. http://www.essdack.org/projects/
- 🌐 Students to the Rescue. http://www.techlearning.com/db_area/archives/WCE/archives/cstevens.htm
- 🌐 The Successful Technology Coordinator. http://www.techlearning.com/db_area/archives/WCE/archives/parham.htm
- 🌐 Teacher Testimony. http://4teachers.org/testimony/archive/index.shtml

Project-Based Learning
- 🌐 Project-Based Learning at a Glance, Edutopia. http://www.glef.org/php/keyword.php?id=037
- 🌐 Project-Based Learning Research, Buck Institute. http://www.bie.org/research/pbl/index.php
- 🌐 Project-Based Learning with Multimedia. http://pblmm.k12.ca.us/
- 🌐 The Road Ahead, ISTE. http://www.iste.org/research/roadahead/pbl.cfm
- 🌐 ThinkQuest. http://www.thinkquest.org/
- 🌐 WebQuest Portal. http://www.webquest.org/

Digital Divide
- 🌐 Center for Applied Special Technology. http://www.cast.org
- 🌐 Digital Divide Network. http://www.digitaldividenetwork.org
- 🌐 Equity Resources, ISTE. http://www.iste.org/resources/equity/index.cfm
- 🌐 Falling Through the Net: Defining the Digital Divide. http://www.ntia.doc.gov/ntiahome/fttn99/contents.html
- 🌐 National Coalition for Equity in Education. http://www.math.ucsb.edu/NCEE
- 🌐 Who's Wired and Who's Not? http://www.futureofchildren.org/usr_doc/vol10no2Art3
- 🌐 World Wide Web Consortium Web Accessibility Initiative. http://www.w3.org/WAI/